100+
GAMES
QUIZZES AND
ICEBREAKERS

100+ GAMES QUIZZES AND ICEBREAKERS

SHIRLEY BLOOMFIELD

MONARCH
BOOKS

Oxford, UK and Grand Rapids, Michigan, USA

First published in the UK in 2008 by Monarch Books
(a publishing imprint of Lion Hudson plc),
Wilkinson House, Jordan Hill Road, Oxford OX2 8DR.
Tel: +44 (0)1865 302750 Fax: +44 (0)1865 302757
Email: monarch@lionhudson.com
www.lionhudson.com

ISBN: 978-1-85424-882-4 (UK)
ISBN: 978-0-8254-6287-0 (USA)

Distributed by:
UK: Marston Book Services Ltd, PO Box 269, Abingdon, Oxon OX14 4YN;
USA: Kregel Publications, PO Box 2607, Grand Rapids, Michigan 49501

British Library Cataloguing Data
A catalogue record for this book is available from the British Library.

Printed and bound in Malta by Gutenberg Press.

INTRODUCTION

There are many occasions in the life of a church (or any social group) when games or entertainment are called for. All too often, however, those to whose lot the organization of such an event falls find themselves at a loss. This book is a collection of tried and tested activities that could prove useful to them. Each of the games is on a separate page to make it easy to photocopy, if needed. Permission to photocopy is included in the price.

From the information given at the top of each page you will quickly be able to decide whether a game is suitable for you. This shows the type of accommodation required (ranging from large hall to small room), the number of players, and the preparation and equipment needed.

The book begins with pencil-and-paper games and moves on to verbal games, musical games and more active games. The last section of the book consists of ideas for entertainment, which guests might enjoy while taking a break from active participation.

While a number of the quizzes are quite suitable for individual contestants, we have often found that people are happier doing them in pairs or in small groups. You will know your own guests and the way they are happiest doing things.

In some of the quizzes there are more questions than you will probably need. They are there to give you more choice, or so that you can eliminate any you feel will be too difficult or irrelevant for your participants. Alternatively, you may have some more topical questions or clues of your own to add.

A few of the quizzes were compiled for special occasions, such as a hog roast, a holiday in Italy, or the millennium. One or two others, rather than being played at a party, were given out to be completed over a longer period during a holiday or an away weekend.

While this book is produced primarily with churches, clubs and social groups in mind, many of the games are equally suitable for smaller family gatherings at home, and there are a number that children will enjoy.

I hope this book will prove a useful resource.

Shirley Bloomfield

ACKNOWLEDGMENTS

While many of these games are my own originals, others are ones devised or organized by other people, which I have played and enjoyed at parties over the years. I am particularly grateful to Mike and Maureen Lawton and John and Liz Sheldon, who kept records of many of the games and loaned me these as a reference. John and Liz also hosted a 'try out new games' evening, which was a great help to me. I would also like to thank friends who have provided such wonderful hospitality over the years for many parties where games have been enjoyed, especially Tony and Ann Nelstrop and Vicki Sirett. Other friends too numerous to mention by name have been very helpful in trying out the various quizzes.

Thanks too to my sister, Jan, who read through many of the pages with a critical eye, suggesting amendments and making constructive suggestions. And my gratitude goes also to my son Martin, and his wife, Sarah, and my other son Paul and his Sarah, who have also given me good ideas and made helpful comments.

Last, but certainly not least, thanks to my husband, Brian, for his encouragement and practical help with day-to-day tasks while his wife was glued to her computer screen!

CONTENTS

1 PARTY PEOPLE

* *NUMBER OF PLAYERS:* Minimum: 20
  Maximum: No limit

* *PLAYED BY INDIVIDUALS*

* *ACCOMMODATION:* Suited to number of players

* *PREPARATION AND EQUIPMENT:* Photocopied list of questions and pen or pencil for each player

* *PLAYERS TO KNOW EACH OTHER WELL:* Not necessary, but preferable

....

A VERY GOOD MIXER FOR THE START OF THE PARTY, TO GET PEOPLE TALKING TO EACH OTHER.

Each player has a list of questions. The answer to each one can be supplied by someone present. Each player goes round asking the questions of other guests and those who can answer 'yes' should sign against the appropriate question. The first person to get a signature against every question is the winner. Here are a few examples that have been used at parties:

1. Who has appeared on television?
2. Who has served in the armed forces?
3. Whose dog ate the Christmas turkey?
4. Who can waggle his/her ears?
5. Who can touch his/her nose with their tongue?
6. Who can speak Japanese?
7. Who has climbed Mount Kilimanjaro?
8. Who has represented his/her country in a sporting event?
9. Who got lost on our trip to Venice?
10. Who met his/her spouse on a blind date?

11. Who has done a parachute jump?
12. Who has a pet snake?
13. Who was born on Christmas Day?
14. Who has met the Queen/President?
15. Who has seen a lion in the wild?
16. Whose hobby is bonsai?
17. Who has had a book published?
18. Who broke her leg skiing?
19. Who is a twin?
20. Who became a grandmother for the first time this year?

2 WHO AM I?

* **NUMBER OF PLAYERS:** Minimum: 15
  Maximum: No limit

* **PLAYED BY INDIVIDUALS**

* **ACCOMMODATION:** Any size of room or hall that can accommodate the number of pairs or individuals playing

* **PREPARATION AND EQUIPMENT:** One or more pads of small 'Post-it®' notes, on each of which is written the name of a well-known person, real or fictional, living or dead. Pack(s) of small adhesive 'spots' (of the type put on paintings in an exhibition to show they are sold)

* **PLAYERS TO KNOW EACH OTHER WELL:** Not necessary

....

ANOTHER GOOD GAME AT THE BEGINNING OF A PARTY, TO GET PEOPLE MIXING.

Players each have one of the named notes stuck on their back.

They then have to go round asking questions of other players to help them identify the name on their back. The answer to their questions can be only 'yes' or 'no'. When they have guessed correctly, they return to the organizer, who will stick another name on their back and also stick a coloured spot to their forehead.

The game goes on for the allotted time (I suggest about 15 minutes) – or until the organizer has run out of adhesive name notes. The winner is the one with the most spots on their forehead.

3 THINGS OUT OF PLACE

* *NUMBER OF PLAYERS:* Minimum: Eight
  Maximum: No limit

* *PLAYED BY INDIVIDUALS OR PAIRS*

* *ACCOMMODATION:* House or hall, allowing all players to roam around without tripping over each other!

* *PREPARATION AND EQUIPMENT:* Pen and paper for each individual or pair. Before people arrive, the organizer will need to go round the house or hall, setting up things that are 'out of place'

* *PLAYERS TO KNOW EACH OTHER WELL:* Not necessary, though it could be helpful

....

THIS GAME NEEDS TO BE PLAYED EARLY ON IN THE GATHERING – IN FACT IT MAKES QUITE A GOOD WARM-UP GAME. IF YOU WAIT TOO LONG, ITEMS WILL GET MOVED AND PEOPLE WILL LEAVE THEIR OWN BELONGINGS AROUND IN A WAY THAT CONFUSES THINGS.

Here are a few suggestions:

When set in a home
- Kitchen or garden items on ornament shelves or in display cabinets
- Last year's calendar on the wall
- Photo of someone (perhaps another guest) that would be unlikely to be on display in this house
- Christmas, Easter or Mother's Day card up at wrong time of year
- Christmas decorations in summer
- Cups, vases or waste bins upside down
- Vegetables in fruit bowl
- Cough mixture bottle among drink bottles

When set in a church hall
- Unlikely book or magazine on bookstall, i.e. *Woman's Own*, *The Beano*, *Reader's Digest*, detective novel
- 'Intruder' among photos of staff or missionaries on noticeboard, e.g. the Queen, the President, the Archbishop of Canterbury, pop star, comedian
- Magazine of another church where church magazines are usually displayed

Either a hall or a house – people
- Woman wearing non-matching earrings
- Man with odd socks
- Woman wearing odd shoes
- Someone with pullover on inside out
- Person with inappropriate badge on (e.g. man – Mothers' Union or Girl Guides)
- Woman with lipstick on lower lip only
- Someone with inappropriate footwear (e.g. wellington boots or fluffy bedroom slippers)
- Watch worn back to front
- Nail varnish on all nails but one

4 PICTURE THE BIBLE BOOK

* *NUMBER OF PLAYERS:* Any number

* *PLAYED BY INDIVIDUALS, PAIRS OR SMALL GROUPS*

* *ACCOMMODATION:* Suited to number of players

* *PREPARATION AND EQUIPMENT:* Sheet of numbered pictures and pen or pencil for each group, pair or individual player

* *PLAYERS TO KNOW EACH OTHER WELL:* Not necessary

....

TRY TO WORK OUT WHICH BOOK OF THE BIBLE THE FOLLOWING PICTURES REPRESENT. WARNING: SOME ARE EXTREMELY CORNY!

1 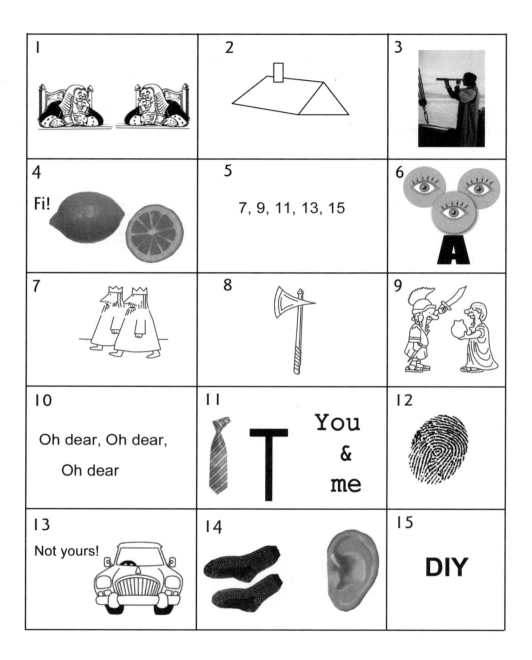	2	3
4 Fi!	5 7, 9, 11, 13, 15	6 A
7	8	9
10 Oh dear, Oh dear, Oh dear	11 T You & me	12
13 Not yours!	14	15 DIY

ANSWERS TO 'PICTURE THE BIBLE BOOK'

1. Judges   2. Ruth   3. Luke   4. Philemon   5. Numbers   6. Isaiah
7. 2 Kings   8. Acts   9. Romans   10. Lamentations   11. Titus
12. Mark   13. Micah   14. Hosea   15. Job

⑤ PET WORDS

* *NUMBER OF PLAYERS:* Any number

* *PLAYED BY INDIVIDUALS, PAIRS OR SMALL GROUPS*

* *ACCOMMODATION:* Suited to number of players

* *PREPARATION AND EQUIPMENT:* Photocopied list and pen or pencil for each group, pair or individual player

* *PLAYERS TO KNOW EACH OTHER WELL:* Not necessary

....

ALL THE ANSWERS TO THE CLUES BELOW BEGIN WITH EITHER THE WORD <u>CAT</u> OR THE WORD <u>DOG</u>. THERE ARE QUITE A FEW MORE 'CATS' THAN 'DOGS'.

1. A Venetian magistrate
2. Turn down page
3. Old naval punishment
4. Firework
5. A drudge
6. Site of bishop's throne
7. Liberal
8. Two-wheeled carriage
9. Worthless and trivial verse
10. To classify
11. Persistent
12. Disaster
13. Intolerantly assertive
14. Instruction by question and answer
15. Waterfall
16. Container for taking home leftovers
17. A mobile launcher
18. Utterly exhausted
19. Underground burial place
20. Two-hulled boat
21. A food provider
22. An unpleasant noise, particularly singing
23. A grub or larva
24. Nasal discharge
25. Swimming stroke

ANSWERS TO 'PET WORDS'

1. Doge
2. Dog-ear
3. Cat o'nine tails
4. Catherine wheel
5. Dogsbody
6. Cathedral
7. Catholic
8. Dog cart
9. Doggerel
10. Catalogue
11. Dogged
12. Cataclysm
13. Dogmatic
14. Catechism
15. Cataract
16. Doggy bag
17. Catapult
18. Dog tired
19. Catacomb
20. Catamaran
21. Caterer
22. Caterwaul
23. Caterpillar
24. Catarrh
25. Doggy paddle

⑥ BODY PARTS

* *NUMBER OF PLAYERS:* Any number

* *PLAYED BY INDIVIDUALS, PAIRS OR SMALL GROUPS*

* *ACCOMMODATION:* Suited to number of players

* *PREPARATION AND EQUIPMENT:* Photocopied list and pen or pencil for each group, pair or individual player

* *PLAYERS TO KNOW EACH OTHER WELL:* Not necessary

....

BELOW ARE CRYPTIC CLUES TO PARTS OF THE HUMAN BODY, WHICH YOU ARE ASKED TO GUESS. IN SOME CASES THE BODY PART WILL NOT BE SPELT THE SAME WAY AS THE ANSWER TO THE CLUE, E.G. 'SPIRITUAL CENTRE OF BEING' – 'SOLE'.

1. Worn by monarch
2. Used in DIY
3. Weapons
4. Top of the hill
5. Surplus disposed of
6. Addition to a book
7. Principal of school
8. Centre
9. Rotten person
10. Animal feet
11. Long-eared mammal
12. Found on a jug
13. Measurement
14. Artists use this
15. Sauce
16. Sticky stuff
17. Found on a shoe
18. Purple flower
19. Part of race
20. Young animal
21. Autumn berry
22. Shellfish
23. Cut of meat
24. Top of wheat
25. Punctuation mark
26. Estuary of river
27. Treasure stored in here
28. Centre of hurricane

ANSWERS TO 'BODY PARTS'

1. Crown
2. Nail
3. Arms
4. Brow
5. Waist
6. Appendix
7. Head
8. Heart
9. Heel
10. Pores
11. Hair
12. Lip
13. Feet
14. Palette
15. Cheek
16. Gum
17. Tongue
18. Iris
19. Lap
20. Calf
21. Hip
22. Muscle
23. Joint
24. Ear
25. Colon
26. Mouth
27. Chest
28. Eye

7 WHICH COUNTRY?

* *NUMBER OF PLAYERS:* Any number

* *PLAYED BY INDIVIDUALS, PAIRS OR SMALL GROUPS*

* *ACCOMMODATION:* Suited to number of players

* *PREPARATION AND EQUIPMENT:* Photocopy of list below and pen or
   pencil for each group, pair or individual player

* *PLAYERS TO KNOW EACH OTHER WELL:* Not necessary

....

FROM THE CLUES BELOW, FIND THE COUNTRY DESCRIBED. SOME ARE VERY CORNY!

Example: Christmas bird = Turkey

1. Mournful sounds
2. Head depot for 'Stop me and buy one'
3. Sounds cold
4. Cups and saucers
5. A popular record label
6. Tree
7. Tries to hurry you
8. In want of a meal
9. Where fresh enthusiasm is found
10. Little Constance (or Conrad) must depart
11. 4,840 square yards of preserve
12. Where they all agree together
13. 'Where the nuts come from'
14. Is Adelaide able to?
15. You must take PAINS for this
16. Prosecute little Daniel
17. A job or vocation
18. Answer to 'How did you get there so quickly?'
19. Get this on for a cross-channel swim
20. Is it a fake? No

ANSWERS TO 'WHICH COUNTRY?'

1. Wales
2. Iceland
3. Chile
4. China
5. Colombia
6. Cyprus
7. Russia
8. Hungry
9. New Zealand
10. Congo
11. Jamaica
12. United States
13. Brazil
14. Canada
15. Spain
16. Sudan
17. Korea
18. Iran
19. Greece
20. Israel

8 WHERE ON EARTH?

* **NUMBER OF PLAYERS:** Any number

* **PLAYED BY INDIVIDUALS, PAIRS OR SMALL GROUPS**

* **ACCOMMODATION:** Suited to number of players

* **PREPARATION AND EQUIPMENT:** Photocopied list of clues and pen or pencil for each group, pair or individual player

* **PLAYERS TO KNOW EACH OTHER WELL:** Not necessary

....

FIND THE ANSWERS TO THE FOLLOWING CLUES TO WELL-KNOWN TOWNS AND CITIES.

1. Dark pond
2. Mythical bird
3. The lady jumps
4. Prevents wet feet
5. Lancasters and Flying Fortresses had one
6. Where to get clean
7. Recently-built fortress
8. The way it's spelt makes it look pleasant
9. Stopper in the bottle
10. Memorial to the dead
11. Increasing in size
12. Harbour or sheltered cove
13. Sprouts
14. Evolutionist
15. Sounds like a wild feline
16. A five-line poem
17. Crimea nurse
18. Prairie beast
19. The Iron Chancellor
20. Hanging decoration
21. He ran off with Helen
22. Orange
23. Female at the anvil
24. 15th-century explorer
25. You can raise the standard here
26. Heavenly being

ANSWERS TO 'WHERE ON EARTH?'

1. Blackpool
2. Phoenix
3. Alice Springs
4. Wellington
5. Bombay
6. Bath
7. Newcastle
8. Nice
9. Cork
10. Tombstone
11. Dublin
12. Anchorage
13. Brussels
14. Darwin
15. Lyon
16. Limerick
17. Florence
18. Buffalo
19. Bismarck
20. Mobile
21. Paris
22. Jaffa or Seville
23. Ladysmith
24. Columbus
25. Flagstaff
26. Archangel

⑨ ON THE MAP

* *NUMBER OF PLAYERS:* Any number, though limited by the number of people available to check the finished papers

* *PLAYED BY INDIVIDUALS OR PAIRS*

* *ACCOMMODATION:* Suited to number of players

* *PREPARATION AND EQUIPMENT:* Photocopied map with questions and pen or pencil for each pair or individual player

* *PLAYERS TO KNOW EACH OTHER WELL:* Not necessary

....

MARK THE STATES ON THE MAP WITH THE NUMBERS GIVEN BELOW (NO NEED TO WRITE THE NAMES).

1. Louisiana
2. West Virginia
3. Idaho
4. Utah
5. Vermont
6. Iowa
7. Wyoming
8. Missouri
9. Florida

10. California
11. Michigan
12. Nebraska
13. Tenessee
14. South Carolina
15. Oklahoma
16. New Mexico
17. Washington
18. Texas

ANSWERS TO 'ON THE MAP'

It won't be possible to call out the answers to this quiz, so someone will need to have been appointed to mark the papers – or, if there is a largish group, two people.

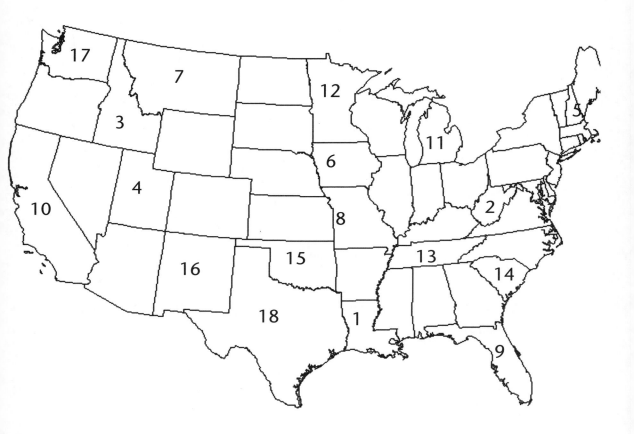

10 WHAT'S ON THE MENU?

* *NUMBER OF PLAYERS:* Any number

* *PLAYED BY INDIVIDUALS, PAIRS OR SMALL GROUPS*

* *ACCOMMODATION:* Suited to number of players

* *PREPARATION AND EQUIPMENT:* Photocopied list and pen or pencil for each group, pair or individual player

* *PLAYERS TO KNOW EACH OTHER WELL:* Not necessary

....

FIND THE DISHES INDICATED BY THE CRYPTIC CLUES BELOW. THE ANSWERS MAY BE PHONETIC RATHER THAN CORRECTLY SPELT, E.G. 'SHARP STICK'. ANSWER: 'STEAK'.

Soup
1. Mother between two toes
2. Fly swisher
3. There's a hole in my bucket

Fish
1. Locality
2. Bride's valued possession
3. Bird's resting place
4. Trade term
5. To glide along

Entrées
1. Nagging woman's weapon
2. Sugared loaf

Game
1. A break in the mountains
2. News carrier
3. Failure to score
4. Woman's crowning glory
5. What a grumbler does

6. Footballer's misdemeanour
7. Middle Eastern country

Meat
1. Eve was made of this
2. Son of Noah
3. An essayist

Dessert
1. Of little importance
2. I cry for help

Vegetables
1. Father using scissors
2. From Scandinavia

Fruit
1. Two of a kind
2. 9 November and 31 December
3. Curse a relation
4. It stuck in Adam's throat
5. Inhabitant of the Antipodes

Drinks
1. Feigned hurt
2. Bacon joint
3. Harbour
4. Strange

ANSWERS TO 'WHAT'S ON THE MENU?'

Soup	1.	Tomato	**Meat**	1.	Spare rib
	2.	Oxtail		2.	Ham
	3.	Leek		3.	Lamb

Fish	1.	Plaice	**Desserts**	1.	Trifle
	2.	Herring		2.	Ice cream
	3.	Perch		3.	Sago
	4.	C.O.D			
	5.	Skate	**Vegetables**	1.	Parsnip
				2.	Swede

Entrées	1.	Tongue			
	2.	Sweetbread	**Fruit**	1.	Pear
				2.	Dates
Game	1.	Partridge		3.	Damson
	2.	Pigeon		4.	Apple
	3.	Duck		5.	Kiwi
	4.	Hare			
	5.	Grouse	**Drinks**	1.	Champagne
	6.	Fowl		2.	Hock
	7.	Turkey		3.	Port
				4.	Rum

11 CUISINE INTERNATIONALE

* *NUMBER OF PLAYERS:* Any number

* *PLAYED BY INDIVIDUALS, PAIRS OR SMALL GROUPS*

* *ACCOMMODATION:* Suited to number of players

* *PREPARATION AND EQUIPMENT:* Photocopied list and pen or pencil for each group, pair or individual player

* *PLAYERS TO KNOW EACH OTHER WELL:* Not necessary

....

ANSWER THESE QUESTIONS ABOUT FOOD AROUND THE WORLD:

1. When a dish is described as 'Florentine', what must it contain?
2. What is the other name for a 'pawpaw'?
3. What are the basic ingredients of 'aloo sag'?
4. What type of flavour does the vegetable fennel have?
5. What type of food was named after Francois-René de Chateaubriand?
6. What is another name for the vegetable 'okra'?
7. What is another name for the Chinese gooseberry?
8. What is 'biltong'?
9. What type of fruit is a 'kumquat'?
10. What name is given to poached and glazed chestnuts?
11. What do we call very young herrings or sprats coated in flour and deep-fried until crisp and golden?
12. What are 'langues de chat'?
13. What would you be eating in New Zealand if you were served with kumara?
14. From which fish does caviar come?
15. What fruit is often served with Parma ham as a first course?
16. What are coquilles St Jacques?

17. When food is cooked 'en croûte', what does it mean?
18. What are prunes wrapped in bacon known as?
19. TVP is a meat substitute. What do the letters stand for?
20. What is the literal meaning of 'chilli con carne'?
21. What is the name for ice cream covered with meringue and baked in the oven?
22. What colour is the pistachio nut?
23. What types of sweets or candy did President Reagan have on his desk?
24. What type of dessert is cassata?

ANSWERS TO 'CUISINE INTERNATIONALE'

1. Spinach
2. Papaya
3. Spinach and potato
4. Aniseed
5. Steak or fillet of beef
6. Ladies' fingers
7. Kiwi fruit
8. Dried meat
9. A small orange
10. Marrons glacés
11. Whitebait
12. A thin biscuit
13. Sweet potato or yams
14. Sturgeon
15. Melon
16. Scallops
17. Wrapped in pastry
18. Devils on horseback
19. Textured vegetable protein
20. Chilli with meat
21. Baked Alaska
22. Green
23. Jelly beans
24. Ice cream

12 HOW MANY?

* **NUMBER OF PLAYERS:** Any number

* **PLAYED BY INDIVIDUALS, PAIRS OR SMALL GROUPS**

* **ACCOMMODATION:** Suited to number of players

* **PREPARATION AND EQUIPMENT:** Photocopied list and pen or pencil for each group, pair or individual player

* **PLAYERS TO KNOW EACH OTHER WELL:** Not necessary

....

FILL IN WORDS FOR THE INITIALS, E.G. 12 D OF C = 12 DAYS OF CHRISTMAS.

1. 3 W M
2. 88 K on a P
3. 7 P of W
4. 1,001 A N
5. 27 B in the N T
6. 64 S on a C B
7. 3 L M from S
8. 13 in a B D
9. 50 S on the U S F
10. 7 A of M
11. 29 D in F in a L Y
12. 10 G B H O T W
13. 1,000 Y in a M
14. 4 H of T A
15. 7 C of the R
16. 3 M in a B
17. 5 L and 2 F
18. 7 C in the B of R
19. 90 D in a R A
20. 7 D in the E C
21. 10 C of the D
22. 5 R on the O F
23. 7 D in S W
24. 15 M on a D M C
25. 26 L of the A
26. 3 L on a S
27. 7 W of the A W
28. 3 C in a F
29. 3,600 S in an H
30. 40 D of L

ANSWERS TO 'HOW MANY?'

1. Wise Men
2. Keys on a piano
3. Pillars of wisdom
4. Arabian Nights
5. Books in the New Testament
6. Squares on a chessboard
7. Little maids from school
8. Baker's dozen
9. Stars on the United States flag
10. Ages of man
11. Days in February in a leap year
12. Green bottles hanging on the wall
13. Years in a millennium
14. Horsemen of the Apocalypse
15. Colours of the rainbow
16. Men in a boat
17. Loaves and fishes
18. Churches in the Book of Revelation
19. Degrees in a right angle
20. Deacons in the early church
21. Cities of the Decapolis
22. Rings on the Olympic flag
23. Dwarfs in Snow White
24. Men on a dead man's chest
25. Letters of the alphabet
26. Leaves on a shamrock
27. Wonders of the ancient world
28. Coins in a Fountain
29. Seconds in an hour
30. 40 days of Lent

13 *TRUE OR FALSE?*

* *NUMBER OF PLAYERS:* Any number

* *PLAYED BY INDIVIDUALS, PAIRS OR SMALL GROUPS*

* *ACCOMMODATION:* Suited to number of players

* *PREPARATION AND EQUIPMENT:* Photocopied list and pen or pencil for each group, pair or individual player

* *PLAYERS TO KNOW EACH OTHER WELL:* Not necessary

....

SAY WHETHER EACH OF THE FOLLOWING STATEMENTS ON THE LIST IS TRUE OR FALSE:

1. Ljubljana is the capital of Slovenia.
2. The book of Job is thought to be the oldest book in the Bible.
3. A pound of lead weighs heavier than a pound of feathers.
4. La Paz is the highest capital city in the world.
5. Revelation is the last book of the Bible.
6. The Great Fire of London was in 1665.
7. Just six people died in the Great Fire of London.
8. The word 'Mornay' describes a dish containing spinach.
9. David wrote the Psalms.
10. Four American presidents have been assassinated...
11. ...and so have two British prime ministers.
12. Auckland is the capital of New Zealand.
13. Two sisters can be fraternal twins.
14. San Marino is the smallest independent state in the world.
15. New York was formerly known as 'Old Antwerp'.
16. Elephants always die when they have lost all their teeth.
17. Crocodiles grow new teeth to replace any they have lost.
18. Leprosy is infectious.
19. Damascus is believed to be the oldest city in the world.

20. The Battle of New Orleans was fought between Britain and the USA.
21. The Hundred Years' War did not last 100 years.
22. Cyprus is the largest island in the Mediterranean.
23. Timothy was the grandson of Eunice.
24. Hippos kill more people than the big cats.
25. Crete is the home of the ancient Etruscan civilization.

If most of the players know each other well, it is more fun if some of the statements can be about people present:

e.g.   The Smiths have been to a Buckingham Palace garden party.
John Jones has appeared on television.
Jane Brown completed the New York marathon.

ANSWERS TO 'TRUE OR FALSE?'

1. True
2. True
3. False (They both weigh the same – 1lb)
4. True
5. False (It should be 'Revelation')
6. False (It was 1666)
7. True
8. False (It means in a cheese sauce)
9. False (He wrote many, but not all of them)
10. True
11. False (Only one has – Spencer Perceval)
12. False (Wellington is the capital)
13. True (Sounds unlikely, but the term 'fraternal' applies to any pair of non-identical twins)
14. False (The Vatican is)
15. False (It was 'New Amsterdam')
16. True
17. True
18. False (It is contagious, which means it can be passed only by direct contact)
19. True
20. True
21. True
22. False (Sicily is)
23. False (Eunice was his mother)
24. True
25. False (The Etruscans lived in Italy)

14 THE LAST CENTURY

* NUMBER OF PLAYERS: Any number

* PLAYED BY INDIVIDUALS, PAIRS OR SMALL GROUPS

* ACCOMMODATION: Suited to number of players

* PREPARATION AND EQUIPMENT: Photocopied list and pen or pencil for each group, pair or individual player

* PLAYERS TO KNOW EACH OTHER WELL: Not necessary

....

COMPLETE THE WORDS TO SHOW WHAT HAPPENED IN THE YEAR IN QUESTION.

 1. 1901 M sends a S across the A
 2. 1903 W B make first F
 3. 1905 A E publishes T of R
 4. 1906 S F E
 5. 1907 B P founds the S
 6. 1912 S of the T
 7. 1913 W W P of the USA
 8. 1914 The O of the P C
 9. 1917 R in R
10. 1919 E R splits the A
11. 1922 D of the T of T
12. 1926 F F around the W
13. 1927 L F the A S
14. 1929 W S C
15. 1932 R E P of USA
16. 1933 H C of G
17. 1938 S W and the S D (W D)
18. 1939 The W O O (M G M)
19. 1941 J A P H

20. 1942 B of S
21. 1944 O O – N L
22. 1945 U N F
23. 1946 N W C tried at N
24. 1947 P E and P P get M
25. 1952 S in the R – G K
26. 1953 C of M E by H and T
27. 1961 B W erected
28. 1962 D of MM
29. 1963 JFK A
30. 1968 D of M L K
31. 1969 F M on T M
32. 1973 W
33. 1974 J C – W C
34. 1975 G F D in S
35. 1980 M S H E
36. 1981 The P is S
37. 1987 TW taken H in B
38. 1991 F G W
39. 1994 1st MRE in SA
40. 1997 D of PD

ANSWERS TO 'THE LAST CENTURY'

1. 1901 *Marconi sends a signal across the Atlantic*
2. 1903 *Wright brothers make first flight*
3. 1905 *Albert Einstein publishes* The Theory of Relativity
4. 1906 *San Francisco earthquake*
5. 1907 *Baden-Powell founds the Scouts*
6. 1912 *Sinking of the* Titanic
7. 1913 *Woodrow Wilson President of the USA*
8. 1914 *The opening of the Panama Canal*
9. 1917 *Revolution in Russia*
10. 1919 *Ernest Rutherford splits the atom*
11. 1922 *Discovery of the tomb of Tutankhamun*
12. 1926 *First flight around the world*
13. 1927 *Lindbergh flies the Atlantic solo*
14. 1929 *Wall Street Crash*
15. 1932 *Roosevelt elected President of USA*
16. 1933 *Hitler Chancellor of Germany*
17. 1938 Snow White and the Seven Dwarfs *(Walt Disney)*
18. 1939 The Wizard of Oz *(MGM))*
19. 1941 *Japan attacks Pearl Harbor*
20. 1942 *Battle of Stalingrad*
21. 1944 *Operation Overlord – Normandy landings*
22. 1945 *United Nations is founded*
23. 1946 *Nazi war criminals tried at Nuremberg*
24. 1947 *Princess Elizabeth and Prince Philip get married*
25. 1952 Singing in the Rain – *Gene Kelly*
26. 1953 *Conquest of Mount Everest by Hillary and Tenzing*
27. 1961 *Berlin Wall erected*
28. 1962 *Death of Marilyn Monroe*
29. 1963 *J. F. Kennedy assassinated*
30. 1968 *Assassination of Martin Luther King*
31. 1969 *First man on the moon*
32. 1973 *Watergate*
33. 1974 *Jimmy Connors – Wimbledon Champion*
34. 1975 *General Franco dies in Spain*
35. 1980 *Mount St Helens erupts*
36. 1981 *The Pope is shot*

37. 1987 Terry Waite taken hostage in Beirut
38. 1991 First Gulf War
39. 1994 First multiracial elections in South Africa
40. 1997 Death of Princess Diana

15 RHYMING PAIRS

* *NUMBER OF PLAYERS:* Any number

* *PLAYED BY INDIVIDUALS, PAIRS OR SMALL GROUPS*

* *ACCOMMODATION:* Suited to number of players

* *PREPARATION AND EQUIPMENT:* Photocopied list and pen or pencil for each group, pair or individual player

* *PLAYERS TO KNOW EACH OTHER WELL:* Not necessary

....

BELOW ARE CLUES TO A TWO-WORD ANSWER THAT RHYMES:

e.g. comical long-eared animal = funny bunny

1. William is pretty stupid
2. Naughty boy
3. Vulgar young man
4. Brilliant illumination
5. Lengthy ditty
6. Enjoyed in upmarket restaurant
7. Equal for all
8. High rate of tax
9. Straight-laced old girl
10. Happy parrot
11. Mickey and Minnie's abode
12. Overweight feline
13. Angry employer
14. Quick meal
15. Clever fellows
16. Suffered on holiday in India
17. To prune the roses
18. Indolent girl
19. Hard to waken from this
20. Unruly infant
21. Fido after his bath
22. Expensive ale
23. Lunch at the inn
24. Hard work on a North Sea rig
25. A terrific friend to have
26. Scientist suffering from respiratory complaint

ANSWERS TO 'RHYMING PAIRS'

1. Silly Billy
2. Bad lad
3. Uncouth youth
4. Bright light
5. Long song
6. Posh nosh
7. Fair share
8. Heavy levy
9. Staid maid
10. Jolly polly
11. Mouse house
12. Fat cat
13. Cross boss
14. Fast repast
15. Wise guys
16. Delhi belly
17. Dead head
18. Lazy Daisy
19. Deep sleep
20. Wild child
21. Wet pet
22. Dear beer
23. Pub grub
24. Oil toil
25. Great mate
26. Coughing boffin

16 *HIDDEN BOOKS OF THE BIBLE*

* *NUMBER OF PLAYERS:* Any number

* *PLAYED BY INDIVIDUALS, PAIRS OR SMALL GROUPS*

* *PREPARATION AND EQUIPMENT:* Photocopied sheet of the passage below
  Pen or pencil for each group, pair or individual player

* *ACCOMMODATION:* Suited to number of players

* *PLAYERS TO KNOW EACH OTHER WELL:* Not necessary

....

FIND 24 BOOKS OF THE BIBLE IN THE FOLLOWING PASSAGE:

I once discovered, merely by a fluke, that many Bible books can be found in ordinary text as long as it is written in Roman script, and I remarked on it to a friend. He had to look very hard to check the facts, but for other people it was a revelation how easy they were to find. One church member, who has as dismal a child as you could ever wish to meet, found it a difficult job. A few of them are difficult and you will feel you are in a real jam, especially as the names of the books were not all capitalized, but the truth was that it was an enjoyable quest. One woman, who saw them at the worst moment of their search, says that she brews a cup of tea to help her concentrate, while I know another who sucks on a humbug to get her through. Another, helping his brain by wearing a fez, raced through them all in no time. He was, of course, from Sudan. I elevated him to the top of the list of fasted winners. John Lightfoot, who lives in Sharp's Almshouses, chose an empty evening to devote to the task and he was working so hard at it that he was up half the night. There are actually 24 books of the Bible in this paragraph, quite a large number, so you may take a little while to complete the whole. In fact I will readily admit it usually takes at least 20 minutes. See how well you can compete. Relaxation is the golden rule and others will judge sympathetically. Yes, there are some that are harder than others to identify and there may be loud lamentations when the last ones are found. I am sure you will find it a most enjoyable exercise.

ANSWERS TO 'HIDDEN BOOKS OF THE BIBLE'

I once discovered, merely by a **fluke**, that many Bible books can be found in ordinary text as long as it is written in **Roman s**cript and I re**mark**ed on it to a friend. He had to look very hard to check the f**acts**, but for other people it was a **revelation** how easy they were to find. One church member, who has as dis**mal a chi**ld as you could ever wish to meet, found it a difficult **job**. A few of them are difficult and you will feel you are in a real **jam, es**pecially as the names of the books were not all capitalized, but the t**ruth** was that it was an enjoyable quest. One woman, who saw the**m at the w**orst moment of their search, says that s**he brews** a cup of tea to help her concentrate, while I know another who sucks o**n a hum**bug to get her through. Another, helping his brain by wearing a **fez, ra**ced through them all in no time. He was, of course, from Su**dan. I el**evated him to the top of the list of fastest winners. **John** Lightfoot, who lives in Shar**p's Alms**houses, chose an empty evening to devote to the task and he was wor**king s**o hard at it that he was up half the night. There are actually 24 books of the Bible in this paragraph, quite a large **number, s**o you may take a little while to complete the whole. In fact I will readily admi**t it us**ually takes at least 20 minutes. See how well you can com**pete. R**elaxation is the golden rule and others will **judge s**ympathetically. **Yes, ther**e are some that are harder than others to identify and there may be loud **lamentations** when the last ones are found. I am sure you will find it **a mos**t enjoyable exercise.

1. Luke	9. Ruth	17. Kings
2. Romans	10. Matthew	18. Numbers
3. Mark	11. Hebrews	19. Titus
4. Acts	12. Nahum	20. Peter
5. Revelation	13. Ezra	21. Judges
6. Malachi	14. Daniel	22. Esther
7. Job	15. John	23. Lamentations
8. James	16. Psalms	24. Amos

17 HIDDEN NAMES OF THOSE PRESENT

* **NUMBER OF PLAYERS:** Minimum: 12
  Maximum: No limit

* **PLAYED BY INDIVIDUALS OR PAIRS**

* **ACCOMMODATION:** Suited to number of players

* **PREPARATION AND EQUIPMENT:** It takes quite a bit of work to write the piece of prose incorporating names of those present (Christian or surname), but, with a bit of thought, this is not too difficult; pens and pencils and photocopied sheets of puzzle to provide one for each team, pair or player

* **PLAYERS TO KNOW EACH OTHER WELL:** Necessary

....

THIS IS REALLY A VARIATION ON THE LAST GAME – FINDING BOOKS OF THE BIBLE HIDDEN IN PROSE.

Here are a few examples of sentences incorporating well-known names:

> It was a cold dar<u>k night</u> (*Knight*).
> The wind was howling in the tree<u>s and ra</u>in (*Sandra*) was driving across the open fields.
> I joined the gym to get fi<u>t. I'm</u> (*Tim*) going there twice a week.

Tip: It is very hard to include any name beginning with 'J'.

18 WHICH HYMN DOES THAT COME FROM?

* **NUMBER OF PLAYERS:** Any number

* **PLAYED BY INDIVIDUALS, PAIRS OR SMALL GROUPS**

* **ACCOMMODATION:** Suited to number of players

* **PREPARATION AND EQUIPMENT:** Photocopied sheet and pen or pencil for each person, pair or group

* **PLAYERS TO KNOW EACH OTHER WELL:** Not necessary

....

BELOW ARE SOME PHRASES FROM WELL-KNOWN CHRISTIAN SONGS AND HYMNS.

Name which ones they are from:

1. …and lips that we might tell
2. …is moving in this place
3. …our faces display your radiance
4. bid my anxious fears subside
5. …but the steep and rugged pathway, may we tread rejoicingly
6. Waste places of Jerusalem…
7. …I scarce can take it in
8. Love so amazing, so divine
9. O perfect redemption
10. Perverse and foolish oft I strayed
11. …gone through the curtain and touching the throne
12. …and point me to the skies
13. The golden evening brightens in the west
14. …till God gives life to the seed
15. …who from our mother's arms

16. well our feeble frame He knows
17. Ye who sang salvation's story
18. …scatters fear and gloom
19. Strength for today and bright hope for tomorrow
20. To reconcile man to God
21. O what peace we often forfeit!
22. …the crown of pain to three and thirty years
23. Humbled for a season
24. …each tree and flower was planned and made
25. But what Thou most desirest, our humble thankful hearts
26. As he died to make men holy…

ANSWERS TO 'WHICH HYMN DOES THAT COME FROM?'

1. All things bright and beautiful
2. Be still, for the presence of the Lord
3. Shine, Jesus, shine
4. Guide me, O Thou great Redeemer
5. Father, hear the prayer we offer
6. Our God reigns
7. How great Thou art
8. When I survey the wondrous cross
9. To God be the glory
10. The King of love my shepherd is
11. Jesus is king and I will extol him
12. Abide with me
13. For all the saints
14. God is working His purpose out
15. Now thank we all our God
16. Praise my soul, the King of heaven
17. Angels from the realms of glory
18. Thine be the glory
19. Great is Thy faithfulness
20. All heaven declares
21. What a friend we have in Jesus
22. I cannot tell why He whom angels worship
23. At the name of Jesus
24. Jesus is Lord
25. We plough the fields and scatter
26. The Battle Hymn of the Republic (Mine eyes have seen the glory)

19 A SONG FOR CHRISTMAS

* *NUMBER OF PLAYERS:* Any number

* *PLAYED BY INDIVIDUALS, PAIRS OR SMALL GROUPS*

* *ACCOMMODATION:* Suited to number of players

* *PREPARATION AND EQUIPMENT:* Photocopied list and pen or pencil for each group, pair or individual player

* *PLAYERS TO KNOW EACH OTHER WELL:* Not necessary

....

NAME THE CHRISTMAS SONG OR CAROL SUGGESTED BY EACH OF THE FOLLOWING DESCRIPTIONS:

1. Bleached Yule
2. Castaneous-coloured seed vesicated in conflagration
3. Singular yearning for the twin anterior incisors
4. Questioning awareness of the season?
5. Arrival time 2400 hrs weather cloudless
6. Loyal followers advance
7. Far off in a feeder
8. Array the corridor
9. Young male percussionist
10. Monarchial triad
11. Nocturnal noiselessness
12. Jehovah deactivate blithe chevaliers
13. Red man en route to borough
14. May frozen precipitation commence
15. Proceed and enlighten on the pinnacle
16. The quadruped with the vermilion proboscis
17. Delight for this planet
18. Give attention for the melodious celestial beings

19. The dozen festive 24-hour intervals
20. Past happening in town of former monarch
21. Flotilla sighted
22. Nocturnal observation by ovine guardians
23. Small equine like quadruped
24. Felicitous sonic tones at altitude
25. Female parent observed in embrace with bearded male

ANSWERS TO 'A SONG FOR CHRISTMAS'

1. White Christmas
2. Chestnuts roasting on an open fire
3. All I want for Christmas is my two front teeth
4. Do they know it's Christmas?
5. It came upon a midnight clear
6. O come, all ye faithful
7. Away in a manger
8. Deck the halls
9. The little drummer boy
10. We three kings
11. Silent night
12. God rest you merry, gentlemen
13. Santa Claus is coming to town
14. Let it snow
15. Go tell it on the mountain
16. The quadruped with the vermillion proboscis
17. Joy to the world
18. Hark the herald angels sing
19. The twelve days of Christmas
20. Once in Royal David's City
21. I saw three ships
22. While shepherds watched
23. Small equine like quadruped
24. Ding dong merrily on high
25. I saw mommy kissing Santa Claus

20 NAME THE TUNE

* **NUMBER OF PLAYERS:** Any number

* **PLAYED BY INDIVIDUALS, PAIRS OR SMALL GROUPS**

* **PREPARATION AND EQUIPMENT:** Prepared tape or CD of about 20 well-known tunes; pen or pencil for each group, team or individual player

* **ACCOMMODATION:** Suited to number of players

* **PLAYERS TO KNOW EACH OTHER WELL:** Not necessary

....

THE TUNES ARE PLAYED ONE AT A TIME AND PEOPLE ARE ASKED TO NAME EACH TUNE.

In some cases, for an extra point, players may also be asked to name the composer or the artist.

21 START THE MUSIC

* *NUMBER OF PLAYERS:* Any number

* *PLAYED BY INDIVIDUALS OR PAIRS*

* *ACCOMMODATION:* Suited to number of players

* *PREPARATION AND EQUIPMENT:* An able pianist or keyboard player, who has prepared in advance; pen or pencil and paper for each individual or pair

* *PLAYERS TO KNOW EACH OTHER WELL:* Not necessary

....

THE PIANIST PLAYS THE FIRST FEW NOTES OF WELL-KNOWN SONGS, HYMNS OR OTHER PIECES OF MUSIC.

The number of notes will depend on how distinctive each tune is.

The players have to write down what they think is the name of each tune.

The one with the most correct answers wins.

22 DUMMIES' MEDICAL DICTIONARY

* *NUMBER OF PLAYERS:* Any number

* *PLAYED IN TEAMS OR BY INDIVIDUALS:* Teams, pairs, or single players

* *ACCOMMODATION:* Suited to number of players

* *EQUIPMENT NEEDED:* Photocopied sheets and pen and paper for each
  person, pair or team

....

*THE LETTERED ITEMS DESCRIBE THE NUMBERED ITEMS. MATCH THE LETTERS TO THE
NUMBERS.*

1. Artery	a.	Back door of a cafeteria
2. Barium	b.	What doctors do when patients die
3. Bacteria		
4. Caesarean section	c.	A punctuation mark
5. Cauterize	d.	Cousin of Elvis
6. Coma	e.	To live longer
7. Dilate	f.	Quicker
8. Enema	g.	Was aware of
9. Fester	h.	A small lie
10. Fibula	i.	The study of painting
11. Labour pain	j.	Getting hurt at work
12. Medical staff	k.	A higher offer
13. Morbid	l.	A person who has fainted
14. Nitrates	m.	Conceited
15. Node	n.	Place to do upholstery
16. Outpatient	o.	Very nearly killed 'em
17. Pap smear	p.	Hiding something
18. Pelvis	q.	Doctor's walking stick
19. Recovery room	r.	Small table
20. Rectum	s.	Not a friend
21. Secretion	t.	A fatherhood test
22. Tablet	u.	Cheaper than day rates
23. Terminal illness	v.	Made eye contact with her
24. Urine	w.	A neighbourhood in Rome
25. Varicose	x.	Getting sick at the airport
26. Vein	y.	Opposite of 'you're out'
	z.	Very near

ANSWERS TO 'DUMMIES' MEDICAL DICTIONARY'

Artery – i

Barium – b

Bacteria – a

Caesarean section – w

Cauterize – v

Coma – c

Dilate – e

Enema – s

Fester – f

Fibula – h

Labour pain – j

Medical staff – q

Morbid – k

Nitrates – u

Node – g

Outpatient – l

Pap smear – t

Pelvis – d

Recovery room – n

Rectum – o

Secretion – p

Tablet – r

Terminal illness – x

Urine – y

Varicose – z

Vein – m

23 MISSING VOWELS

❋ **NUMBER OF PLAYERS:** Any number

❋ **PLAYED BY INDIVIDUALS, PAIRS OR SMALL GROUPS**

❋ **ACCOMMODATION:** Suited to number of players

❋ **PREPARATION AND EQUIPMENT:** Photocopied list and pen or pencil for each group, pair or individual player

❋ **PLAYERS TO KNOW EACH OTHER WELL:** Not necessary

....

BELOW IS A LIST OF FILM TITLES WITH ALL VOWELS, PUNCTUATION AND SPACES REMOVED. TRY TO WORK OUT WHAT THEY ARE.

1. NGLDNPND
2. CRSL
3. DDPTSSCTY
4. DRVMGMSSDSY
5. TFFRCA
6. SVNGPRVTRYN
7. BRDGTFR
8. GNWTHTHWND
9. SHN
10. HGHSCTY
11. THBRDMNFLCTRZ
12. LRDFTHRNGS
13. PNNCH
14. STRDYNGHTFVR
15. BLLNDTDSXCLLNTDVNTR
16. BCKTTHFTR
17. MTTMNSTLS
18. MDRNTMS
19. NTHWTRFRNT
20. RBELWTHTCS
21. SNSTBLVRD
22. GNTLMNPRFRBLNDS
23. GRLWTHPRLRRNG
24. TRSRSLND
25. LCENWNDLND
26. DMNDSRFRVR
27. NTHBCH
28. TRGRT
29. LCDSNTLVHRNYMR
30. GRS

ANSWERS TO 'MISSING VOWELS'

1. On Golden Pond
2. Carousel
3. Dead Poets Society
4. Driving Miss Daisy
5. Out of Africa
6. Saving Private Ryan
7. A Bridge Too Far
8. Gone with the Wind
9. Shane
10. High Society
11. The Birdman of Alcatraz
12. Lord of the Rings
13. Pinocchio
14. Saturday Night Fever
15. Bill and Ted's Excellent Adventure
16. Back to the Future
17. Meet Me in St Louis
18. Modern Times
19. On the Waterfront
20. Rebel without a Cause
21. Sunset Boulevard
22. Gentlemen Prefer Blondes
23. Girl with a Pearl Earring
24. Treasure Island
25. Alice in Wonderland
26. Diamonds are Forever
27. On the Beach
28. True Grit
29. Alice Doesn't Live Here Any More
30. Grease

24 TREBLE CHANCE

* *NUMBER OF PLAYERS:* Any number

* *PLAYED BY INDIVIDUALS, PAIRS OR SMALL GROUPS*

* *ACCOMMODATION:* Suited to number of players

* *PREPARATION AND EQUIPMENT:* Photocopied list and pen or pencil for each group, pair or individual player

* *PLAYERS TO KNOW EACH OTHER WELL:* Not necessary

....

FIND THE THIRD WORD TO ADD TO THE PAIRS LISTED BELOW:

e.g. Tom, Dick and ???? – answer: 'Harry'.

1. Hook, line and?
2. Crosby, Hope and?
3. Lies, damned lies and?
4. Faith, hope and?
5. Caspar, Melchior and?
6. Peter, Paul and?
7. The long, the short and?
8. Bell, book and?
9. Coin, sheep and?
10. Latvia, Lithuania and?
11. Bacon, lettuce and?
12. Queen, worker and?
13. Doric, Ionian and?
14. Shadrach, Meshach and?
15. Majorca, Minorca and?
16. Hatched, matched and?
17. Athos, Porthos and?

18. Kenya, Uganda and?
19. The good, the bad and the?
20. Truly, madly,…?
21. Proton, neutron and?
22. Slugs and snails and.?
23. Wine, women and?
24. Bewitched, bothered and?
25. Carreras, Domingo and?
26. Foil, epée and?
27. *East of Eden*, *Rebel without a Cause* and?
28. Nina, Pinta and?
29. Acute, obtuse and?
30. The world, the flesh and?

ANSWERS TO 'TREBLE CHANCE'

1. Sinker
2. Lamour
3. Statistics
4. Charity or love
5. Balthazar
6. Mary (1960s folk song trio)
7. The tall (song title and film title)
8. Candle
9. Son (parables of things lost)
10. Estonia (the three 'Baltic States')
11. Tomato (popular sandwich filling)
12. Drone
13. Corinthian (Greek styles of columns)
14. Abednego
15. Ibiza (the Balearic Islands)
16. Despatched
17. Aramis (3 musketeers)
18. Tanganyika (former British colonies in East Africa linked together)
19. Ugly
20. Truly, madly, deeply (Film title)
21. Electron
22. Puppy dogs' tails (Rhyme 'What are little boys made of?')
23. Song
24. Bewildered (words of a song)
25. Pavarotti (the three tenors)
26. Sabre (fencing swords)
27. Giant (James Dean's three films)
28. Santa Maria (Columbus's ships)
29. Reflex (angles)
30. The Devil

25 LINKS

* *NUMBER OF PLAYERS:* Any number

* *PLAYED BY INDIVIDUALS, PAIRS OR SMALL GROUPS*

* *ACCOMMODATION:* Suited to number of players

* *PREPARATION AND EQUIPMENT:* Photocopied list and pen or pencil for each group, pair or individual player

* *PLAYERS TO KNOW EACH OTHER WELL:* Not necessary

....

THE SETS OF WORDS BELOW ARE ALL LINKED IN SOME WAY. IT MAY BE A GROUP TERM, OR A WORD THAT CAN BE PLACED BEFORE OR AFTER EACH ONE IN THE GROUP:

e.g. Gerald, Richard, Ronald, Bill, George (US presidents),
or gage, land, peace (can be prefixed with the word 'green').

1. Cat, dog, angel, jelly, gold
2. Betty, Fred, Wilma, Barney
3. Apes, cedarwood, sandalwood, peacocks
4. Katherine, Anne, Jane, Anne, Catherine
5. Morocco, Singapore, Hong Kong, Mandalay
6. Patience, Mabel, Buttercup, Tessa
7. Stanley, Rackstraw, Murgatroyd, Oakapple
8. Jig, bow, chain, circular
9. Gandhi, Sadat, Rabin, McKinley
10. John, William, Miles, Martin
11. Tax, compact, slipped, floppy
12. Melbourne, Rome, Tokyo, Barcelona, Munich
13. Black, Red, Dead, Irish
14. *Oklahoma!, The Sound of Music, The King and I, Flower Drum Song*

15. Martin, Thomas, Lucia, Bartholomew
16. Ham, cheese, violets
17. Benedict, Paul, John, Julius, Leo
18. Margaret, Tony, Jim, John
19. Michael, Michael, Eddie, Richard
20. Anne, Branwell, Emily, Charlotte
21. Martin, Nicholas, Edwin, Oliver
22. Draw, suspension, contract, swing
23. Columbus, Austin, Raleigh, Quincy, Jackson
24. Painted, Thar, Great Sandy, Simpson
25. Bob, Jacob, Tim, Ebenezer
26. Geoffrey, Michael, Donald, Robert, George
27. Sean, Roger, Timothy, Pierce
28. Kariba, Aswan, Möhne, Hoover
29. Liesl, Friedrich, Marta, Gretel, Kurt, Brigitta,
30. Wright, Johnson, Brown, Mollison, Alcock

ANSWERS TO 'LINKS'

1. Fishes
2. Flintstones
3. Goods carried in the poem Cargoes by John Masefield
4. Wives of Henry VIII
5. Road films
6. Female characters in Gilbert and Sullivan operas
7. Male characters in Gilbert and Sullivan operas
8. Types of saw
9. World leaders who have been assassinated
10. Bible translators
11. Discs
12. Cities in which the Olympics have been held
13. Seas
14. All Rodgers and Hammerstein musicals
15. They are all Caribbean islands if the prefix 'St' is added
16. All products from city of Parma in Italy
17. Popes
18. British prime ministers
19. Husbands of Elizabeth Taylor
20. The Brontë family
21. Dickens title characters
22. Bridges
23. American cities
24. Deserts
25. Characters in Dickens' A Christmas Carol
26. Archbishops of Canterbury
27. Have all played James Bond
28. Dams
29. Von Trapp children
30. Aviators

26 ODD MAN OUT

* NUMBER OF PLAYERS: Any number

* PLAYED BY INDIVIDUALS, PAIRS OR SMALL GROUPS

* ACCOMMODATION: Suited to number of players

* PREPARATION AND EQUIPMENT: Photocopied list and pen or pencil for each group, pair or individual player

* PLAYERS TO KNOW EACH OTHER WELL: Not necessary

....

ONE WORD IN EACH GROUP DOESN'T BELONG:

e.g. apple, grape, banana, turnip, strawberry, orange. Answer: turnip (the only one not a fruit but a vegetable).

Find the odd one out in each group:

1. Typhoon, hurricane, tornado, mistral, monsoon, chinook
2. North, Red, Coral, Dead, China, Gulf
3. Isaiah, Amos, Solomon, Jeremiah, Hosea, Nahum
4. Terrier, Dalmatian, Bulldog, Harrier, Whippet
5. Peter, Stephen, Andrew, Paul, John
6. Rommel, Montgomery, Eisenhower, Patten, Slim, McArthur
7. Bangkok, Teheran, Colombo, Jakarta, Islamabad, Calcutta
8. Mars, Venus, Jupiter, Saturn, Neptune
9. Eroica, New World, Pastoral, Mars
10. Nutmeg, mace, ginger, thyme, cinnamon, turmeric
11. Mumbai, Islamabad, Calcutta, Delhi, Madras
12. Eagle, kestrel, kite, robin, condor, falcon
13. Malvolio, Bassanio, Oberon, Cordelia, Calaban, Francesco
14. Juno, Mars, Neptune, Diana, Poseidon, Mercury

15. Melbourne, Halifax, Darwin, Perth, Brisbane
16. Wheat, oats, soya, rice, maize
17. Ephesians, Corinthians, Romans, Philemon, Galatians
18. Columbus, Cortes, Scott, Hudson, Nelson, Cabot
19. Hampshire, Mexico, York, Jersey, Georgia
20. Matthew, Peter, Thomas, Philip, Mark
21. French, German, Spanish, Italian, Romanian
22. Mushroom, truffle, toadstool, puffball, champignon
23. Mickey, Donald, Pluto, Jerry, Thumper
24. Prussian, cobalt, ultramarine, crimson, turquoise
25. Femur, tibia, clavicle, biceps, sternum
26. Namibia, Bhutan, Zambia, Niger, Gambia
27. Oboe, flute, clarinet, bassoon, trombone
28. Doe, lamb, calf, fawn
29. Parsnip, cabbage, carrot, turnip, sweet potato
30. April, June, July, September, November

ANSWERS TO 'ODD MAN OUT'

1. Monsoon: the others are all winds, whereas the monsoon is simply the wet season
2. Gulf: the only one not the name of a sea
3. Solomon: the only one not a prophet
4. Dalmatian: the only one without double letters in its spelling
5. John: the only one who didn't suffer a martyr's death
6. Rommel: he was a German general. The rest were from the Allied Nations
7. Calcutta: the others are all capital cities
8. Venus: the only planet named after a female god
9. Jupiter: the only one not a symphony
10. Thyme: thyme is a herb. The rest are spices
11. Islamabad: the only city in Pakistan, not India
12. Robin: the only one not a bird of prey
13. Francesco is the only one not a Shakespearean character
14. Poseidon was a Greek god. The others were Roman
15. Halifax: the only one not an Australian state capital
16. Soya: the only one not a cereal
17. Philemon: the only epistle in the group addressed to one person rather than a group
18. Nelson: he was the only one not an explorer, but an admiral
19. Georgia: the only one not a US state if prefixed by the word 'New'
20. Mark: the only one not one of the 12 apostles
21. German: the only non-Latin-based language
22. Toadstool: the only non-edible fungus
23. Jerry: the only non-Disney cartoon character
24. Crimson: the only colour not a shade of blue
25. Biceps: this is a muscle, while the rest are all bones
26. Bhutan: the only country in Asia, not Africa
27. Trombone: the only brass instrument
28. Doe: the only one not a young or baby animal
29. Cabbage: the only one not a root vegetable
30. July: the only month with 31 days

27 THE ITALIAN JOB

* NUMBER OF PLAYERS: Any number

* PLAYED BY INDIVIDUALS, PAIRS OR SMALL GROUPS

* ACCOMMODATION: Suited to number of players

* PREPARATION AND EQUIPMENT: Photocopied list of questions and pen or pencil for each group, team or individual player

* PLAYERS TO KNOW EACH OTHER WELL: Not necessary

....

THIS QUIZ WAS DEVISED FOR A GROUP HOLIDAY IN ITALY.

Similar ones could be worked out for other countries.

1. For what three things is the town of Parma famous?
2. What is the longest river in Italy?
3. What was Mussolini's first name?
4. In which year did he come to power?
5. What do the Italians call the city we know as Florence?
6. Who were Marco and Giuseppe Palmieri?
7. In what field was Maria Montessori a pioneer?
8. What is the name of the strait that separates Italy from Sicily?
9. 'All over Italy you hear his concertina.' To whom does this line in a song refer?
10. There are two small states surrounded by Italian territory. Name them both.
11. What term do the Italians use for spaghetti that is just ready to eat and hasn't got too soggy?
12. Name the two leading actors in the film *Roman Holiday*.
13. Where did Gracie Fields own a villa?
14. On what river does Rome stand?

15. If a dish is described as 'Florentine', what must it contain?
16. By what name was Angelo Roncalli better known?
17. Who composed the opera *Aida*?
18. We call it a motorway; the Germans call it an 'autobahn'. What do the Italians call it?
19. What was the name of the famous monastery that was the site of a great battle in World War II?
20. What did the puppet maker Gepetto create?
21. St Francis of Assisi founded the Franciscan friars. Who founded the sister order for women?
22. What is the name of the mountain range that goes down the centre of Italy?
23. What does the term 'La dolce vita' mean?
24. What event of note happened in AD 79?
25. Which Italian patriot had a biscuit or cookie named after him?
26. What is the name of the fountain in Rome into which tourists throw coins?
27. What is the meaning of the opera title *Il Trovatore*?
28. What are the Italian equivalents of the following English names:
    - John?
    - Joseph?
    - Peter?
    - Paul?
    - Charles?

ANSWERS TO 'THE ITALIAN JOB'

1. Ham, cheese and violets
2. The Po
3. Benito
4. 1922
5. Firenze
6. The two gondoliers in the Gilbert and Sullivan opera The Gondoliers
7. Nursery education
8. Messina
9. Poppa Piccolina
10. The Vatican and San Marino
11. Al dente'
12. Gregory Peck and Audrey Hepburn
13. Capri
14. The Tiber
15. Spinach
16. Pope John XXIII
17. Verdi
18. Autostrada
19. Monte Cassino
20. Pinocchio
21. St Clare
22. The Apennines
23. The sweet life
24. Vesuvius erupted, destroying Pompeii
25. Garibaldi
26. Trevi
27. The Troubadour
28. Giovanni
    Giuseppe
    Pietro
    Paolo
    Carlo

28 HOG ROAST QUIZ

❋ *NUMBER OF PLAYERS:* Any number

❋ *PLAYED BY INDIVIDUALS OR PAIRS*

❋ *ACCOMMODATION:* Suited to number of players

❋ *PREPARATION AND EQUIPMENT:* Photocopied list of questions and pen or pencil and paper for each individual or pair

❋ *PLAYERS TO KNOW EACH OTHER WELL:* Not necessary

....

THE FOLLOWING QUIZ WAS USED AT A HOG ROAST PARTY, BUT OF COURSE IT CAN BE USED FOR ANY OCCASION.

All the questions below have connections with pigs.

1. What was Piglet's favourite food?
2. Whose friend was Podgy Pig?
3. Which city in northern Italy is famous for its ham?
4. Finish this saying: 'Cats are your superiors, dogs are your inferiors and pigs are…'
5. Which pig had 'a ring at the end of his nose'?
6. What name is given to the herd of pigs into which Jesus sent the evil spirits from Legion? 'The … Swine.'
7. From which country does the potbellied pig come?
8. What was the name of the chief pig in *Animal Farm*?
9. … and what was the name of his banished arch-rival?
10. What is the French word for ham?
11. … and what is the German word for ham?

12. Give the next line of this verse:

   'This little piggy went to market;
   This little piggy stayed at home;
   This little piggy had...

13. In which novel did a boy whose name was Piggy feature?
14. ... and who wrote it?
15. Which fictional pig found fame as a 'sheepdog'?
16. Pigs are used to hunt for special luxury foods. What are they?
17. One Beatrix Potter story was about a pig. What was it called?
18. Of what does the dish 'Pigs in blankets' consist?
19. Name a breed of pig beginning with T.
20. Who was so hungry he wanted to eat the husks fed to pigs?
21. Which religion beside Judaism forbids eating pork?
22. What do we call a pig in its wild state?

ANSWERS TO 'HOG ROAST QUIZ'

1. Acorns
2. Rupert Bear
3. Parma
4. Your equals
5. *The pig in* The Owl and the Pussycat
6. *The Gadarene Swine*
7. Vietnam
8. Napoleon
9. Snowball
10. Jambon
11. Schinken
12. Roast beef
13. Lord of the Flies
14. William Golding
15. Babe
16. Truffles
17. The Tale of Pigling Bland
18. Oysters wrapped in bacon
19. The Tamworth
20. The prodigal son
21. Islam
22. Boar

29 HAPPY CHRISTMAS

* *NUMBER OF PLAYERS:* Any number

* *PLAYED BY INDIVIDUALS, PAIRS OR SMALL GROUPS*

* *ACCOMMODATION:* Suited to number of players

* *PREPARATION AND EQUIPMENT:* Photocopied list and pen or pencil for each group, pair or individual player

* *PLAYERS TO KNOW EACH OTHER WELL:* Not necessary

....

1. When was the first Christmas card sent: a.1810 b.1832 c.1843 d.1867?
2. What is the carol 'Adeste Fideles' known as in English?
3. What are the traditional names of the three Wise Men?
4. 'Santa Claus' is a derivative of the name of which Christian saint?
5. What was the gift sent on the tenth day of Christmas?
6. When does Russia celebrate Christmas Day?
7. What is the date of St Nicholas' day?
8. St Nicholas was a bishop in the early church. Bishop of where?
9. By what name is ilex better known?
10. In the Book 'A Christmas Carol' what was the name of Scrooge's dead partner
11. Which saint does legend say chopped down a pagan sacred oak and chose an evergreen fir as a symbol of the Christ child (i.e. the first Christmas tree)
12. Which English ruler abolished Christmas?
13. What province of South Africa was named for Christmas Day, when the explorer Bartholomew Diaz landed there?
14. What connection has Franz Gruber with Christmas?
15. Who wept for her children in Ramah?

16. Which prophet foretold that Jesus would be born in Bethlehem?
17. Who painted the picture 'The Massacre of the Innocents'?
18. The song 'I'm dreaming of a White Christmas' was first heard in a 1942 black and white film. What was the film called?
19. The season just before Christmas is called Advent. What does the word 'advent' mean?
20. In the poem 'The Night before Christmas', what is the name of the next reindeer – Dasher, Dancer, Prancer and ???
21. With which day is the Lord of Misrule or the Boy Bishop associated?
22. Which saint's day is celebrated the day after Christmas Day?
23. And which saint is commemorated on 27 December?
24. Where and when was the Christmas truce?
25. What is the name of the most famous Christmas ballet?

ANSWERS TO 'HAPPY CHRISTMAS'

1. 1843
2. O come, all ye faithful
3. Melchior, Caspar and Balthazar
4. St Nicholas
5. Ten lords a leaping
6. 6 January
7. 6 December
8. Myra
9. Holly
10. Jacob Marley
11. Boniface
12. Oliver Cromwell
13. Natal
14. He composed the carol 'Silent night'
15. Rachel
16. Micah
17. Rubens
18. Holiday Inn
19. Coming
20. Vixen
21. 6 January, Twelfth Night or the Feast of the Epiphany
22. St Stephen
23. St John the Apostle
24. Christmas Day 1914, when Germans and British temporarily stopped fighting and went out to meet each other
25. The Nutcracker

30 PAIR UP

* NUMBER OF PLAYERS: Any number

* PLAYED BY INDIVIDUALS, PAIRS OR SMALL GROUPS

* ACCOMMODATION: Suited to number of players

* PREPARATION AND EQUIPMENT: Photocopied list and pen or pencil for each group, pair or individual player

* PLAYERS TO KNOW EACH OTHER WELL: Not necessary

···

BELOW IS A LIST OF PAIRS OF WORDS. JUST THE FIRST LETTER OF EACH WORD IS GIVEN, AND EACH DOT REPRESENTS A LETTER.

e.g. R . . . . and J . . . . . (Romeo and Juliet)   or   h . . . and m . . . . . (high and mighty)

1. P . . . . and B . . .
2. S . . . . . and D . . . . . .
3. G . . . . . and S . . . .
4. L . . . . and C . . . .
5. G . . . and D . . . .
6. C . . . . . and C . . . .
7. J . . . . . and H . . .
8. A . . . . and B . . . .
9. D . . . . and B . . . .
10. R . . . . . and H . . . .
11. A . . . . and P . . . .
12. C . . . . and P . . . .
13. P . . . and B . . . .
14. S . . . . and M . . . .
15. M . . . . and P . . . .

16. J . . . and J . . . .
17. L . . . . . and H . . . .
18. B . . . . . and C . . . .

1. f . . . and f . . . . . .
2. t . . . . and e . . . .
3. b . . . . and w . . . .
4. n . . . . . . and c . . . . . .
5. k . . . and k . .
6. h . . and t . . . .
7. p . . . . and s . . .
8. e . . and s . . . .
9. w . . . and w . . .
10. b . . . . and b . . . . .
11. p . . . . and p . . . .
12. n . . and t . . .
13. t . . . and t . . .
14. h . . . and m . . . . .
15. b . . . . and b . . . .
16. s . . . . and b . . . .
17. b . . . . and t . . . . .
18. s . . . . and s . . . .

ANSWERS TO 'PAIR UP'

1. Porgy and Bess
2. Samson and Delilah
3. Gilbert and Sullivan
4. Lewis and Clark
5. Guys and Dolls
6. Caesar and Cleopatra
7. Jekyll and Hyde
8. Alcock and Brown
9. David and Bathsheba
10. Rodgers and Hammerstein
11. Aquila and Priscilla
12. Castor and Pollux
13. Paul and Barnabas
14. Sankey and Moody
15. Medes and Persians
16. John and James
17. Laurel and Hardy
18. Bonnie and Clyde

1. Fast and furious
2. Trial and error
3. Black and white
4. Noughts and crosses
5. Kith and kin
6. Hip and thigh
7. Pepper and salt
8. Egg and spoon
9. Warp and weft
10. Bread and butter
11. Powers and principalities
12. Nip and tuck
13. Time and tide
14. High and mighty
15. Bright and beautiful
16. Skin and bone
17. Block and tackle
18. Short and sweet

31 OTHERWISE KNOWN AS...

* *NUMBER OF PLAYERS:* Any number

* *PLAYED BY INDIVIDUALS, PAIRS OR SMALL GROUPS*

* *ACCOMMODATION:* Suited to number of players

* *PREPARATION AND EQUIPMENT:* Photocopied list and pen or pencil for each group, pair or individual player

* *PLAYERS TO KNOW EACH OTHER WELL:* Not necessary

....

WHAT WERE THE REAL NAMES OF THE FOLLOWING?

1. The Scarlet Pimpernel
2. Old Blood and Guts
3. The Lady of the Lamp
4. Boz
5. The Old Groaner
6. The White Queen of Calabar
7. The Merry Monarch
8. The Swedish Nightingale
9. Satchmo
10. The Sun King
11. The Maid of Orleans
12. Ol' Blue Eyes
13. The Sons of Thunder
14. Didymus
15. Boney
16. The Swan of Avon

AS WHOM WERE THE FOLLOWING BETTER KNOWN?

1. Agnes Gonxha Bojaxhiu
2. Eric Arthur Blair
3. St Nicholas of Myra
4. Vladimir Ilyich Ulyanov
5. Airman T. E. Shaw
6. Iosif Vissarionovich Dzhugashvili
7. Archibald Alexander Leach
8. Norma Jean Baker
9. Martha Jane Cannary-Burke
10. Mary Mallon
11. Ivan IV
12. Adolf Schickelgruber
13. Josip Broz
14. Robert Stroud
15. William Cody
16. Bernard Schwartz

ANSWERS TO 'OTHERWISE KNOWN AS ...'

What were the real names of the following?

1. Percy Blakeney
2. General George Patten
3. Florence Nightingale
4. Charles Dickens
5. Bing Crosby
6. Mary Slessor
7. Charles II
8. Jenny Lind
9. Louis Armstrong
10. Louis XIV of France
11. Joan of Arc
12. Frank Sinatra
13. James and John
14. Thomas the Apostle
15. Napoleon Bonaparte
16. William Shakespeare

As whom were the following better known?

1. Mother Teresa
2. George Orwell
3. Santa Claus or Father Christmas
4. Lenin
5. Lawrence of Arabia
6. Stalin
7. Cary Grant
8. Marilyn Monroe
9. Calamity Jane
10. Typhoid Mary
11. Ivan the Terrible
12. Adolf Hitler
13. Tito
14. The Birdman of Alcatraz
15. Buffalo Bill
16. Tony Curtis

32 TRANSATLANTIC TRANSLATION

* *NUMBER OF PLAYERS:* Any number

* *PLAYED BY INDIVIDUALS, PAIRS OR SMALL GROUPS*

* *ACCOMMODATION:* Suited to number of players

* *PREPARATION AND EQUIPMENT:* Photocopied list and pen or pencil for each group, pair or individual player

* *PLAYERS TO KNOW EACH OTHER WELL:* Not necessary

....

WHICH WORDS DO AMERICANS USE FOR THE FOLLOWING ENGLISH WORDS?

1. Nappy
2. Puncture
3. Pavement
4. Cornflour
5. Solicitor
6. Maths
7. Braces
8. Engine driver
9. Vest
10. 2nd-year university student
11. Aubergine
12. Queue
13. Bill
14. Shop
15. Garden
16. Draughts
17. Pack of cards

WHICH WORDS DO THE BRITISH USE FOR THE FOLLOWING AMERICAN WORDS?

1. Hood
2. Trunk
3. Freeway
4. Chips
5. Flashlight
6. Sneakers
7. Cookie
8. Jelly
9. Jello
10. Faucet
11. Stroller
12. Streetcar
13. Gasoline
14. Antenna
15. Vest
16. Teeter totter
17. First floor

ANSWERS TO 'TRANSATLANTIC TRANSLATION'

1. Diaper
2. Blowout
3. Sidewalk
4. Cornstarch
5. Lawyer
6. Math
7. Suspenders
8. Engineer
9. Singlet
10. Sophomore
11. Eggplant
12. Line
13. Check
14. Store
15. Yard
16. Checkers
17. Deck of cards

1. Bonnet
2. Boot
3. Motorway
4. Potato crisps
5. Torch
6. Plimsolls or gym shoes
7. Biscuit
8. Jam
9. Jelly
10. Tap
11. Pushchair
12. Tram
13. Petrol
14. Aerial
15. Waistcoat
16. Seesaw
17. Ground floor

33 WHICH BOOK?

* *NUMBER OF PLAYERS:* Any number

* *PLAYED BY INDIVIDUALS, PAIRS OR SMALL GROUPS*

* *ACCOMMODATION:* Suited to number of players

* *PREPARATION AND EQUIPMENT:* Photocopied list of questions and pen or pencil for each group, pair or individual player

* *PLAYERS TO KNOW EACH OTHER WELL:* Not necessary

....

IN WHICH BOOK OR BOOKS ARE THE FOLLOWING CHARACTERS FOUND?

1. Tom Joad
2. Bathsheba Everdene
3. Noah Claypole
4. Atticus Finch
5. Ashley Wilkes
6. Mrs Danvers
7. Anne Shirley
8. Maurice Vaughan
9. Touchstone
10. Alan Breck
11. Allan Quatermain
12. Mrs Hudson
13. Simon Legree
14. John Brooke
15. Mr J. L. B. Matekoni
16. Tinkerbell
17. Maggie Tulliver
18. Holden Caulfield
19. Eustace Scrubbs
20. Mrs Malaprop
21. Joe Harman
22. Judith Starkadder
23. Selina Cross
24. Hubert Lane
25. Mr Bingley
26. Tigger

ANSWERS TO 'WHICH BOOK?'

1. *The Grapes of Wrath*
2. *Far From the Madding Crowd*
3. *Oliver Twist*
4. *To Kill a Mockingbird*
5. *Gone with the Wind*
6. *Rebecca*
7. *The 'Anne of Green Gables' books*
8. *The 'Whiteoaks of Jalna' books*
9. *As You Like It*
10. *Kidnapped*
11. *King Solomon's Mines* or *Allan Quatermain*
12. *'Sherlock Holmes' books*
13. *Uncle Tom's Cabin*
14. *Little Women*
15. *The No. 1 Ladies Detective Agency*
16. *Peter Pan and Wendy*
17. *The Mill on the Floss*
18. *The Catcher in the Rye*
19. *The 'Narnia' books,* particularly *The Voyage of the Dawn Treader*
20. *The Rivals*
21. *A Town like Alice*
22. *Cold Comfort Farm*
23. *Peyton Place*
24. *The 'Just William' books*
25. *Pride and Prejudice*
26. *Winnie the Pooh* or *The House at Pooh Corner*

34 *WHO SAID THAT?*

* *NUMBER OF PLAYERS:* Any number

* *PLAYED BY INDIVIDUALS, PAIRS OR SMALL GROUPS*

* *ACCOMMODATION:* Suited to number of players

* *PREPARATION AND EQUIPMENT:* Photocopied list of questions and pen or pencil for each group, pair or individual player

* *PLAYERS TO KNOW EACH OTHER WELL:* Not necessary

....

WHO IS REPUTED TO HAVE SAID THE FOLLOWING?

1. 'The reports of my death have been greatly exaggerated'
2. 'Religion is the opium of the people'
3. 'Patriotism is not enough'
4. '..a workman not ashamed'
5. 'Give us the tools and we will finish the job'
6. 'Why should the devil have all the best tunes?'
7. 'To die would be an awfully big adventure'
8. 'The buck stops here'
9. 'I have the heart of a king'
10. 'I shall be late, I shall be late'
11. 'Dr Livingstone, I presume'
12. 'My brother is a hairy man'
13. 'Why don't they eat cake?'
14. 'I have a dream'
15. 'Ich bin ein Berliner'
16. 'Are there no workhouses?'
17. '… a date which will live in infamy'
18. 'Is this a dagger which I see before me?'
19. 'Give me a child until he is seven and I will give you the man'

20. 'I shall return'
21. 'Mine eyes have seen Thy salvation'
22. 'The world is my parish'
23. 'Christmas won't be Christmas without any presents'
24. 'When a man is tired of London, he is tired of life'
25. 'I am the greatest'

ANSWERS TO 'WHO SAID THAT?'

1. Mark Twain
2. Karl Marx
3. Edith Cavell
4. Paul to Timothy
5. Winston Churchill
6. General William Booth
7. Peter Pan
8. Harry S. Truman
9. Queen Elizabeth I
10. The white rabbit in Alice in Wonderland
11. Henry Stanley
12. Jacob
13. Marie Antoinette
14. Martin Luther King
15. John F. Kennedy
16. Scrooge
17. Lady Macbeth
18. The Jesuits
19. General Douglas MacArthur
20. President Franklin D. Roosevelt
21. Simeon
22. John Wesley
23. Jo in Little Women
24. Dr Samuel Johnson
25. Muhammad Ali

35 NAME THE ARTIST

✳ *NUMBER OF PLAYERS:* Any number

✳ *PLAYED BY INDIVIDUALS, PAIRS OR SMALL GROUPS*

✳ *ACCOMMODATION:* Suited to number of players

✳ *PREPARATION AND EQUIPMENT:* Photocopied list and pen or pencil for each group, pair or individual player

✳ *PLAYERS TO KNOW EACH OTHER WELL:* Not necessary

....

WHO PAINTED THE FOLLOWING? YOU ARE NOT EXPECTED TO GET BOTH THE FIRST NAME AND THE SURNAME.

1. The Cornfield
2. The Night Watch
3. The Bombing of Guernica
4. Christ of St John of the Cross
5. Girl with a Pearl Earring
6. Peasants Dancing at a Wedding
7. The Last Supper
8. The Mona Lisa
9. Bubbles
10. Derby Day
11. The Light of the World
12. The Rake's Progress
13. Two Tahitian Women
14. Bathers by the River
15. The Scream
16. The Blue Boy
17. The Monarch of the Glen
18. The Fighting Téméraire
19. Moulin Rouge
20. The Poppy Field
21. Praying Hands
22. The Laughing Cavalier
23. Sunflowers
24. The Birth of Venus
25. The ceiling of the Sistine Chapel

ANSWERS TO 'NAME THE ARTIST'

1. John Constable
2. Rembrandt
3. Pablo Picasso
4. Salvador Dali
5. Johannes Vermeer
6. Brueghel
7. Leonardo da Vinci
8. Leonardo da Vinci
9. J. E. Millais
10. William Powell Frith
11. William Holman Hunt
12. William Hogarth
13. Paul Gauguin
14. Renoir
15. Edvard Munch
16. Thomas Gainsborough
17. Edwin Landseer
18. William Turner
19. Henri de Toulouse Lautrec
20. Claude Monet
21. Albrecht Dürer
22. Franz Hals
23. Vincent van Gogh
24. Botticelli
25. Michelangelo

36 WHAT'S THAT, DOC?

* NUMBER OF PLAYERS: Any number

* PLAYED BY INDIVIDUALS, PAIRS OR SMALL GROUPS

* ACCOMMODATION: Suited to number of players

* PREPARATION AND EQUIPMENT: Photocopied list of questions and pen or pencil for each group, team or individual player

* PLAYERS TO KNOW EACH OTHER WELL: Not necessary

....

HERE IS A LIST OF MEDICAL CONDITIONS. MOST OF US KNOW THEM BY A MORE MUNDANE NAME.

Write this name against as many of the words as you can,

e.g. Rubella – German measles.

1. Variola
2. Varicella
3. Alopecia
4. Caries
5. Rubeola
6. Dyspepsia
7. Contusion
8. Strabismus
9. Pertussis
10. Urticaria
11. Parotitis
12. Tinea pedis
13. Consumption
14. Seasonal allergic rhinitis
15. Hyperglycaemia
16. Hypoglycaemia
17. Quinsy
18. Myopia
19. Hypertension
20. Necrosis
21. Myocardial infarction
22. Hansen's Disease
23. Gingivitis
24. Calculus

ANSWERS TO 'WHAT'S THAT, DOC?'

1. Smallpox
2. Chickenpox
3. Hair loss
4. Tooth decay
5. Measles
6. Indigestion
7. Bruise
8. Squint
9. Whooping cough
10. Nettle rash or hives
11. Mumps
12. Athlete's foot
13. Tuberculosis
14. Hay fever
15. High blood sugar
16. Low blood sugar
17. Tonsillitis
18. Short-sightedness
19. High blood pressure
20. Dead skin or tissue
21. Heart attack
22. Leprosy
23. Inflammation and infection of the gums
24. Kidney or bladder stone

37 ANAGRAMS OF BIBLICAL CHARACTERS

* *NUMBER OF PLAYERS:* Any number

* *PLAYED BY INDIVIDUALS, PAIRS OR SMALL GROUPS*

* *ACCOMMODATION:* Suited to number of players

* *PREPARATION AND EQUIPMENT:* Photocopied list and pen or pencil for each group, pair or individual player

* *PLAYERS TO KNOW EACH OTHER WELL:* Not necessary

....

BELOW IS A LIST OF ANAGRAMS OF BIBLICAL CHARACTERS. THEY MAY INCLUDE THE WORDS 'THE' OR 'OF':

1. ABHSTABEH
2. AIJMEEHR
3. USMDCOINE
4. LLGMEAAI
5. SBBAABRA
6. NAJAHNTO
7. HHSEETMULA
8. ITITITTEHRUAHHE
9. IPPOLTNUISTAE
10. ZAABSRLHEZ
11. OYMITHT
12. JALHEI
13. BAELGRI
14. LBOASMA
15. AEEIHMHN
16. CSRAAHDH
17. GAYNMEDEALMRA
18. WEMOTHBORAL
19. MSYNEEFIOCNRO
20. BZLEEJE
21. TEAAIAFOOHPJERMHS
22. LPPIIH

ANSWERS TO 'ANAGRAMS OF BIBLICAL CHARACTERS'

1. Bathsheba
2. Jeremiah
3. Nicodemus
4. Gamaliel
5. Barabbas
6. Jonathan
7. Methuselah
8. Uriah the Hittite
9. Pontius Pilate
10. Belshazzar
11. Timothy
12. Elijah
13. Gabriel
14. Absalom
15. Nehemiah
16. Shadrach
17. Mary Magdalene
18. Bartholomew
19. Simon of Cyrene
20. Jezebel
21. Joseph of Arimathea
22. Philip

38 SORT OUT THE SAINTLY

* *NUMBER OF PLAYERS:* Any number

* *PLAYED BY INDIVIDUALS, PAIRS OR SMALL GROUPS*

* *ACCOMMODATION:* Suited to number of players

* *PREPARATION AND EQUIPMENT:* Photocopied list and pen or pencil for each group, pair or individual player

* *PLAYERS TO KNOW EACH OTHER WELL:* Not necessary

....

BELOW ARE ANAGRAMS OF SAINTS OR WELL-KNOWN CHRISTIANS DOWN THE AGES.

In the case of actual saints the word 'saint' or the letters 'St' are not included, but the word 'of' may be included, e.g. 'Joseph of Arimathea'.

1. HRLOOWBATEM
2. SSSSRIIFCNAIOAF
3. GYMMELERAADAN
4. RUEEEBOTRSLTNFOADDE
5. MGYLAABRILH
6. TUEGASNUI
7. VLEOVGNAIISDIDTN
8. CRJNAAOFO
9. WARDEN
10. PPLIIH
11. YLOSHDATORUN
12. RMERSOAETTHE
13. ENSEPHT
14. OTEOINMBORCRE
15. BNAAL
16. TEANSITAN
17. GSUYLLTOAINAIO
18. WHUIINFNROOCJLA
19. YZURKCINC
20. CAPTKIR
21. HLSOINCA
22. TNIVLANEE
23. OREEGG
24. ASABANBR

ANSWERS TO 'SORT OUT THE SAINTLY'

1. Bartholomew
2. Francis of Assisi
3. Mary Magdalene
4. Bernadette of Lourdes
5. Billy Graham
6. Augustine
7. David Livingstone
8. Joan of Arc
9. Andrew
10. Philip
11. Hudson Taylor
12. Mother Teresa
13. Stephen
14. Corrie ten Boom
15. Alban
16. Nate Saint
17. Ignatius Loyola
18. Julian of Norwich
19. Nicky Cruz
20. Patrick
21. Nicholas
22. Valentine
23. George
24. Barnabas

39 FOR ALL THE SAINTS

* *NUMBER OF PLAYERS:* Any number

* *PLAYED BY INDIVIDUALS, PAIRS OR SMALL GROUPS*

* *ACCOMMODATION:* Suited to number of players

* *PREPARATION AND EQUIPMENT:* Photocopy of list and pen or pencil for each group, pair or individual player

* *PLAYERS TO KNOW EACH OTHER WELL:* Not necessary

....

ALTHOUGH MANY PEOPLE WILL NOT BE AWARE OF MOST OF THESE PATRON SAINTS, IT IS SURPRISING HOW MANY CAN BE WORKED OUT WITH A LITTLE THOUGHT.

Who are the patron saints of the following countries listed below?
1. France
2. Wales
3. Russia
4. Greece
5. Italy

… and of which country are each of the following the patron saint?
1. Francis Xavier
2. Stanislaus
3. Olaf

… and who are the patron saints of the following?
1. Hopeless cases or lost causes
2. Accountants
3. Soldiers
4. Grocers
5. Doctors

6. Unmarried women
7. Travellers
8. Hairdressers
9. Musicians
10. Dancing
11. Animals
12. Lovers
13. Against snake bite
14. Fishermen
15. Pawnbrokers
16. Fathers
17. Lost Property

ANSWERS TO 'FOR ALL THE SAINTS'

Patron saints of countries:
1. Joan of Arc/Denis
2. David
3. Basil/Nicholas
4. George
5. Francis of Assisi/Catherine of Siena

Which country has this patron saint?
1. India
2. Poland
3. Norway

Who are the patron saints of the following groups of people?
1. Jude
2. Matthew
3. Joan of Arc
4. Michael
5. Luke
6. Nicholas
7. Christopher
8. Mary Magdalene
9. Cecilia
10. Vitus
11. Francis of Assisi
12. Valentine
13. Paul
14. Peter
15. Nicholas
16. Joseph
17. Anthony of Padua

 SHOPPING TRIP

* **NUMBER OF PLAYERS:** Any number

* **PLAYED BY INDIVIDUALS, PAIRS OR SMALL GROUPS**

* **ACCOMMODATION:** Suited to number of players

* **PREPARATION AND EQUIPMENT:** Quite a lot of preparation is needed for this game. On a visit to the local shopping centre, the organizer will take pictures of the logos or descriptions (e.g. 'Everything for the man about town' or 'All your sporting requirements') on shop fronts. These will be reproduced on a sheet with each photo numbered; photocopied sheets of logos in local shopping centre; Pen and paper for each person, pair or group

* **PLAYERS TO KNOW EACH OTHER WELL:** Not necessary

....

ASK THE PLAYERS TO NAME AS MANY SHOPS AS THEY CAN IDENTIFY FROM THE LOGOS AND/OR DESCRIPTIONS ON THEIR SHEET.

BABY OR CHILDHOOD PHOTOS

* **NUMBER OF PLAYERS:** Minimum of 12
  Maximum: No limit – but the majority should be known to one another

* **PLAYED IN PAIRS OR AS INDIVIDUALS**

* **ACCOMMODATION:** Suited to number of players

* **PREPARATION AND EQUIPMENT:** Photos, numbered and displayed; pen and paper

* **PLAYERS NEED TO KNOW EACH OTHER WELL:** Necessary

....

BEFORE THE DAY, COLLECT PHOTOS OF 10–20 PEOPLE WHO WILL BE PRESENT, TAKEN WHEN THEY WERE EITHER BABIES OR FAIRLY YOUNG CHILDREN.

Number these and either display them around the room or pass them round.

Players have to guess whom each photo portrays.

42 FACIAL FEATURES

* **NUMBER OF PLAYERS:** Minimum: 15
  Maximum: 30

* **PLAYED AS INDIVIDUALS**

* **ACCOMMODATION:** Suited to number of players

* **PREPARATION AND EQUIPMENT:** Photos of all or most of those present, which have been cropped on the computer, leaving just either the eyes or the mouth; each one to be numbered and stuck on the wall; alternatively, if there is a comparatively small number playing, the numbered pictures can be passed round the room to each player in turn; pen and paper for each player

* **PLAYERS TO KNOW EACH OTHER WELL:** Necessary

....

THE AIM IS FOR THE PLAYERS TO IDENTIFY AS MANY AS POSSIBLE OF THOSE PRESENT FROM THE PHOTOS.

43 GET IT WRITE

* **NUMBER OF PLAYERS:** Any number

* **PLAYED BY INDIVIDUALS OR PAIRS**

* **ACCOMMODATION:** Suited to number of players

* **PREPARATION AND EQUIPMENT:** Copy of printed passage and pen and paper for each individual or pair

* **PLAYERS TO KNOW EACH OTHER WELL:** Not necessary

....

IN THE FOLLOWING PASSAGE THERE ARE 28 ERRORS. THEY MAY BE SPELLING, GRAMMATICAL OR FACTUAL.

Players should mark what is wrong and number and explain each error on their blank sheet of paper.

St Peters' Church run a number of homegroups, which are usually comprised of between 10 and 15 members, although some have less.

Most of them follow a series of Bible studies covering both the Old and New Testaments. Recently they have studied Exodus, Hezekiah, Thessallonians, Matthew and Revelations. One of the aims as they study a passage is to try to see it's relevance to modern everyday life.

Most groups also organize a number of social events. One very successful recent one was an Itialian evening. First they enjoyed a meal of gazpacho followed by either tagliatele Milanese or lasagne, with tiramisu for desert.

Another group often runs travel evenings, when members talk about their holidays and show slides of where they have been. They have been to many exiting places. Jane Smith went out to Kenya to climb Killimanjaro and the Weston family went on a trek to the sumit of Cotopaxi in Bolivia. Of course foreign travel has its hazards, although the likelihood of visitors contracting anything serious can be considerably reduced by the appropriate vacinations. For instance when young Jonathan Rice went backpacking on the Indian subcontinent he made sure he had his typhoid, hepititis and yellow fever jabs first, although they were not able to protect him from the altitude sickness he suffered in Kathmandu, Nepal. We cannot emphasize too strongly that people didn't ought to travel to third world countries without first taking professional medical advice.

A number of members are interested in golf, both as active players and as armchair adicts. Sometimes they find it more fun for a number of them to get together to watch a match in someones' home, as they did recently for the Wightman Cup. The more active guys dream of the day when they reach the necessary standard to compete for the Curtis Cup.

SOLUTIONS TO 'GET IT WRITE'

1. **St Peters'** Church 2. **run** a number of homegroups, which are usually 3. **comprised of** between 10 and 15 members, although some have 4. **less.** Most of them follow a series of Bible studies covering both the Old and New Testaments. Recently they have studied Exodus, 5. **Hezekiah**, 6. **Thessallonians**, Matthew and 7. **Revelations**. One of the aims as they study a passage is to try to see 8. **it's** relevance to modern everyday life.

Most groups also organize a number of social events. One very successful recent one was an 9. **Itialian** evening. First they enjoyed a meal of 10. **gazpacho** followed by either 11. **tagliatele** Milanese or lasagne, with tiramisu for 12. **desert**.

Another group often runs travel evenings, when members talk about their holidays and show slides of where they have been. They have been to many 13. **exiting** places. Jane Smith went out to 14. **Kenya** to climb 15. **Killimanjaro**, whilst the Weston family went on a trek to the 16. **sumit** of 17. **Cotopaxi** in 18. **Bolivia**. Of course foreign travel has its hazards, although the likelihood of visitors contracting anything serious can be considerably reduced by the appropriate 19. **vacinations**. For instance, when young Jonathan Rice went backpacking on the Indian subcontinent he made sure he had his typhoid, 20. **hepititis** and 21. **yellow fever** jabs first, although they were not able to protect him from the 22. **altitude sickness** he suffered in Kathmandu, Nepal. We cannot emphasize too strongly that people 23. **didn't ought** to travel to third-world countries without first taking professional medical advice.

A number of members are interested in golf, both as active players and as armchair 24. **adicts**. Sometimes they find it more fun for a number of them to get together 25. **to watch a match in 26. someones**' home, as they did recently for the 27. **Wightman Cup**. The more active guys dream of the day when they reach the necessary standard to compete for the 28. **Curtis Cup**.

1. *St Peters' Church: apostrophe in wrong place. It should be 'St Peter's'.*
2. *Should be 'St Peter's Church "runs"', as the word 'Church' is singular.*
3. *It shouldn't be 'comprised of' but 'comprising'.*
4. *The word 'less' is incorrect – it should be 'fewer'.*
5. *Hezekiah – there is no book of Hezekiah.*
6. *Thessallonians – spelt wrongly. It should be 'Thessalonians'.*
7. *Revelation – not Revelations.*
8. *it's. There should not be an apostrophe here. It should be 'its'.*
9. *Itialian – spelling. Should be 'Italian'.*
10. *Gazpacho is Spanish, not Italian.*
11. *Tagliatele – spelling. Should be 'tagliatelle'.*
12. *Dessert, not 'desert'.*
13. *Exciting, not exiting.*
14. *Kilimanjaro is in Tanzania, not Kenya.*
15. *...and it should be spelt with only one 'l': 'Kilimanjaro'.*
16. *'sumit' should be 'summit'.*
17. *They were unlikely to have climbed Cotopaxi – it is an active volcano!*
18. *And it is in Ecuador, not Bolivia.*
19. *Vacinations should be 'vaccinations'.*
20. *'Hepititis' is spelt wrongly – it should be 'hepatitis'.*
21. *Yellow fever: you don't need yellow fever jabs for Asia, only for Africa and South America.*
22. *You won't get altitude sickness in Kathmandu – it's only 1,344m or 4,445ft above sea level.*
23. *People didn't ought – should be 'ought not'.*
24. *'Adicts' spelt wrongly – it should be 'addicts'.*
25. *Insert 'on TV' – they don't watch the actual match in a home!*
26. *'Someones'' – apostrophe in wrong place. It should be 'someone's'.*
27. *Wightman Cup – This is a tennis cup, not golf.*
28. *The Curtis Cup – the guys can't compete. It's a ladies' tournament!*

 DINGBATS 1

* **NUMBER OF PLAYERS:** Any number

* **PLAYED BY INDIVIDUALS, PAIRS OR SMALL GROUPS**

* **ACCOMMODATION:** Suited to number of players

* **PREPARATION AND EQUIPMENT:** Photocopied sheet of dingbats and pen or pencil for each group, team or individual player

* **PLAYERS TO KNOW EACH OTHER WELL:** Not necessary

....

1 Proc eedings	**2** Sweeping – pweesing Weesping – weepings Swingeep – sweeping	**3** Trductiono
4 Hopes Hopes Hopes Hopes Hopes	**5** Shopping around bargain bargain bargain bargain	**6** Mexican
7 Owt2027	**8** T U R N	**9** **Safety** Comfort Value Enjoyment
10 **Standing** **miss**	**11** THEGOTHE	**12** Falling
13 T12"omb	**14** Tacles Tacles Tacles Tacles tacles Tacles Tacles Tacles tacles Tacles	**15** TUNNEL
16 Responsibility	**17** Happeningyyyyyyyy	**18** Miss Jones Mrs Brown Lady Angela Dame Margaret
19 Society	**20** 1	**21** TALL

ANSWERS TO 'DINGBATS 1'

1. A gap in the proceedings
2. Sweeping changes
3. Introduction
4. Fading hopes
5. Shopping around for bargains
6. Mexican wave
7. Back to the future
8. Turn right
9. Safety first
10. Misunderstanding
11. The go-between
12. Falling off the edge
13. One foot in the grave
14. Tentacles
15. Light at the end of the tunnel
16. Diminished responsibility
17. Wise after the happening
18. Little women
19. High society
20. A hole in one
21. Walk tall

45 *DINGBATS 2*

* *NUMBER OF PLAYERS:* Any number

* *PLAYED BY INDIVIDUALS, PAIRS OR SMALL GROUPS*

* *ACCOMMODATION:* Suited to number of players

* *PREPARATION AND EQUIPMENT:* Photocopied sheet of dingbats and pen or pencil for each group, team or individual player

* *PLAYERS TO KNOW EACH OTHER WELL:* Not necessary

....

1 pals, chums, mates (in circle)	2 G N I breath M breath O breath C breath	3 GSGE
4 ~~FOR THE SHORE~~	5 SYMPHON	6 Ange
7 stretch hcterts	8 PERSONALITY	9 Not hing
10 Harmon iiiiiiiii	11 CHICKEN 12	12 Cutting
13 LOAD LOAD LOAD	14 folly 4" 3" 2" 1"	15 B E MANNER D
16 (lines)	17 worl	18 YoCu
19 PAL	20 head LO heels VE	21 lookkoolcrossing

ANSWERS TO 'DINGBATS 2'

1. Circle of friends
2. Coming up for breath
3. Scrambled eggs
4. Strike out for the shore
5. Unfinished symphony
6. Archangel
7. Two-way stretch
8. Split personality
9. Nothing is black and white
10. Harmonize
11. Cheaper by the dozen
12. Cutting edge
13. Lighten the load
14. Height of folly
15. Bedside manner
16. On the right lines
17. World without end
18. See through you
19. Checkmate
20. Head over heels in love
21. Look both ways before crossing

 46 DINGBATS 3

* **NUMBER OF PLAYERS:** Any number

* **PLAYED BY INDIVIDUALS, PAIRS OR SMALL GROUPS**

* **ACCOMMODATION:** Suited to number of players

* **PREPARATION AND EQUIPMENT:** Photocopied sheet of dingbats and pen or pencil for each group, team or individual player

* **PLAYERS TO KNOW EACH OTHER WELL:** Not necessary

....

1 `1 3 5 7 9` **ALL**	**2** *HEARTED*	**3** EXIT **leg**
4 POTOOOOOOOO	**5** i i i i	**6** CEPS CEPS CEPS CEPS
7 Y N N U S	**8** YOUJUSTME	**9** hand **mouth** **mouth**
10 Amsterdam The Hague Jan van Eyck Joost van Haagen	**11** hicken	**12** **L✗east**
13 B a t t e r y	**14** **ZZZ** **TASK**	**15** K K C C U U T T S S WORD WORD WORD WORD
16 **ICE³**	**17** Hurri **i** cane	**18** **Clever** ½ **Clever**
19 aerobics aerobics aerobics aerobics	**20** France Germany France Germany Australia Australia China China	**21** LSSBGNIES

ANSWERS TO 'DINGBATS 3'

1. Against all the odds
2. Faint-hearted
3. Go out on a limb
4. Potatoes
5. Eyes right
6. Forceps
7. Sunny side up
8. Just between you and me
9. Hand to mouth
10. Double Dutch
11. Headless chicken
12. Last but not least
13. Flat battery
14. Asleep on the job
15. Too stuck up for words
16. Ice cube
17. Eye of the hurricane
18. Too clever by half
19. Step aerobics
20. Shadowlands
21. Mixed blessings

 **LET'S FACE IT (FAMOUS FACES)**

✴ *NUMBER OF PLAYERS:* Minimum: Six
Maximum: No limit

✴ *PLAYED BY INDIVIDUALS, PAIRS OR SMALL GROUPS*

✴ *ACCOMMODATION:* Enough room for all present

✴ *PREPARATION AND EQUIPMENT:* Photos of well-known people, each one to be numbered or pasted on the wall, and pen or pencil and paper for each person, group or pair

THE PICTURES CAN BE EITHER PASSED ROUND TO PLAYERS OR DISPLAYED ON THE WALLS AROUND THE ROOM, AND THE PLAYERS WRITE DOWN WHO THEY THINK EACH PERSON IS.

48 HOLIDAY DESTINATIONS

* *NUMBER OF PLAYERS:* Any number

* *PLAYED BY INDIVIDUALS OR PAIRS*

* *ACCOMMODATION:* Suited to number of players

* *PREPARATION AND EQUIPMENT:* Pictures of holiday destinations, cut out of travel brochures and magazines, with any relevant wording cut off or covered over. Each one is to be numbered and stuck on the wall; alternatively, if there is a comparatively small number playing, the numbered pictures can be passed round the room to each player in turn; pencil and paper for each player or pair of players

* *PLAYERS TO KNOW EACH OTHER WELL:* Not necessary

••

THE PLAYERS ARE ASKED TO NAME EACH HOLIDAY DESTINATION.

The amount of time allowed will depend on the number of players and how long they feel they need.

The winner is the one naming the most destinations correctly.

 **KIM'S GAME**

* *NUMBER OF PLAYERS:* Minimum: Six
                                              Maximum: 30

* *PLAYED BY INDIVIDUALS*

* *ACCOMMODATION:* Suited to number of players

* *PREPARATION AND EQUIPMENT:* A tray set out with about 20–25 objects
      Pen or pencil and paper for each player

* *PLAYERS TO KNOW EACH OTHER WELL:* Not necessary

....

THE PRESET TRAY IS BROUGHT IN, COVERED BY A CLOTH, AND PLACED WHERE ALL THE PLAYERS CAN SEE IT. IT IS UNCOVERED, LEFT THERE FOR THREE MINUTES AND THEN COVERED AGAIN.

The players then have to write down all the objects they can remember and the one who has remembered the most is the winner.

Players probably need about five minutes for this.

Some suggestions for objects to be placed on the tray:

• Paper clip
• Cotton reel
• Pen or pencil
• Toothbrush or nailbrush
• Hairbrush or comb
• Paintbrush
• Scissors
• Item of cutlery

- Lipstick
- Bottle of perfume
- Biscuit or cookie
- Rubber band
- Nail file or emery board
- Piece of jewellery
- Peppermill
- Diary
- Tea bag
- Piece of fruit
- Torch or flashlight
- Feather
- Tweezers
- Postage stamp
- Nut
- Drinking straw
- Egg cup
- Eraser
- Tin opener, bottle opener or corkscrew
- Cork

50 *WHAT DOES IT FEEL LIKE?*

* *NUMBER OF PLAYERS:* Minimum: Six
  Maximum: Multiples of groups of six

* *PLAYED BY INDIVIDUALS*

* *ACCOMMODATION:* Suited to number of players

* *PREPARATION AND EQUIPMENT:* For each group of six a plastic or brown paper bag filled with about 20 different small objects (the same contents for each group); pen or pencil and paper for each player

* *PLAYERS TO KNOW EACH OTHER WELL:* Not necessary

....

THIS IS REALLY A VARIATION ON KIM'S GAME, BUT IN THIS ONE THE PLAYERS FEEL FOR THE OBJECTS IN A BAG, PUTTING THEIR HANDS RIGHT INSIDE, BUT NOT LOOKING.

Give them 30 seconds to feel around and then either ring a bell or call out 'Pass it on'. When everyone has had a feel around a bag, they should all try to write down as many as they can identify and can remember.

Suggestions for content of bags:

1. Paper clip
2. Safety pin
3. Bulldog clip
4. Pencil or pen
5. Envelope
6. Spoon
7. Apple
8. Orange or lemon

9. Cork or bottle stopper
10. Candle
11. Walnut
12. Drinking straw
13. Roll of sticky tape
14. Dried kidney bean
15. Torch or flashlight
16. Comb
17. Rubber band
18. Cotton bud
19. Sock
20. Glove
21. Emery board
22. Piece of cotton wool
23. Piece of string
24. Button
25. Reel of cotton
26. Tea bag
27. Piece of celery
28. Carrot
29. Dried kidney bean
30. Coin

51 SNIFF IT OUT

* *NUMBER OF PLAYERS:* Minimum: Six
                      Maximum: Multiples of groups of six

* *PLAYED BY INDIVIDUALS*

* *ACCOMMODATION:* Suited to number of players

* *PREPARATION AND EQUIPMENT:* For each group of six a number (suggest about 15) of small pill boxes or film containers filled with different substances that can be identified by smell; each group to have the same set of substances; pen or pencil and paper for each player

* *PLAYERS TO KNOW EACH OTHER WELL:* Not necessary

....

THE SMALL CONTAINERS ARE PASSED ONE AT A TIME ROUND EACH GROUP FOR THE PLAYERS TO SNIFF WHILE THEY HAVE THEIR EYES SHUT.

Once they have passed a container to the person on their left, they should write down the substance they think it contained.

Suggestions for contents of the containers. Some of the following:

1. Tea
2. Coffee (instant or beans)
3. Chocolate powder
4. Grated lemon rind
5. Soap or detergent
6. Brown sugar (has a more distinctive smell than white)
7. Jam
8. Marmalade
9. Honey

10. Mayonnaise
11. Tomato ketchup
12. Almond essence
13. Marmite or Vegemite
14. Toothpaste
15. Cloves
16. Coriander seeds
17. Caraway seeds
18. Dried thyme
19. Mint leaves
20. Rosemary
21. Peanut butter
22. Disinfectant
23. Mustard
24. Slice of banana

52 GET YOUR MIND ROUND THIS

* *NUMBER OF PLAYERS:* Any number

* *PLAYED BY INDIVIDUALS*

* *ACCOMMODATION:* Suited to number of players

* *PREPARATION AND EQUIPMENT:* Pen and pencil and paper for each player

* *PLAYERS TO KNOW EACH OTHER WELL:* Not necessary

....

The organizer says:

'I am going to ask you thee questions
and you have to answer them instantly.
You can't take your time – you have to answer immediately.
Let's find just how clever you really are

Ready?

First question
You are participating in a race.
You overtake the second.
In what position do you finish?
Write it down quickly.

Answer
If you answer that you arrived first, then you are absolutely wrong!!!
Because if you overtake the second and you take his place, then you arrived second.

Second question
If you overtake the last then you arrive...?
Write it down quickly.

Answer
If you answer that you arrived second last, then you are wrong again.
Tell me, how can you overtake the LAST??
The question is wrong!
You're not very good at this, are you???

Third question
This has to be done in your head. No pencil and paper.

Take 1,000 and add 40 to it.
Now add another 1,000.
Now add 30.
Another 1,000.
Now add 20.
Now add another 1,000.
Now add 10.

What is the total?
Did you get 5,000?
The correct answer is actually 4,100.
Don't believe it? Check it.

53 NOT SO OBVIOUS – BRAINTEASERS

* NUMBER OF PLAYERS: Any number

* PLAYED BY INDIVIDUALS OR PAIRS

* ACCOMMODATION: Suited to number of players

* PREPARATION AND EQUIPMENT: Photocopied list of questions and pen or pencil for each player or pair

* PLAYERS TO KNOW EACH OTHER WELL: Not necessary

....

1. If I take two apples from three apples, what do I have?
2. A farmer had 17 sheep. All but nine died. How many did he have left?
3. If you had only one match and entered a room in which there was a kerosene lamp, a gas ring and a fuel stove, what would you light first?
4. If you went to bed at 8 o'clock and set the alarm to go off at 9 o'clock the next morning, how many hours' sleep would this let you have?
5. A man builds a house with four sides to it and it is rectangular in shape, each side having a southerly aspect. A big bear walks past. What colour is the bear?
6. How many animals of each species did Moses take into the ark?
7. How many months of the year have 28 days?
8. If you drive a bus with 43 persons on board from Chicago and stop at Pittsburgh to pick up seven more people and drop off five passengers and at Cleveland drop off eight passengers and pick up four more, and eventually arrive at Philadelphia 20 hours later, what is the name of the driver?

9. Which country has the 4th July, Britain or America?
10. If a doctor gives you three pills and tells you to take one every half hour, how long would it be before all the pills are used up?
11. Is it legal in Britain and the USA for a man to marry his widow's sister?
12. An archaeologist claims he has found two coins dated BC46? Would they be genuine?
13. How many birthdays does the average man have?
14. Why can't a man living in Newcastle be buried west of York?

ANSWERS TO 'NOT SO OBVIOUS — BRAINTEASERS'

1. Two apples – you took that number!
2. Nine
3. The match
4. One hour
5. White – because the house would have to be at the North Pole
6. None – Moses didn't go into the ark!
7. All of them
8. Your own name
9. Both
10. One hour
11. If he has a widow, he is dead and so can't remarry!
12. No. No one used the dates 'BC' until after the birth of Jesus
13. 1. The same date each year
14. Because if he is <u>living</u> in Newcastle he won't need to be buried yet!

54 LETTER PYRAMID

* *NUMBER OF PLAYERS:* Minimum: Six
  Maximum: No limit

* *PLAYED BY INDIVIDUALS OR PAIRS*

* *ACCOMMODATION:* Suited to number of players

* *PREPARATION AND EQUIPMENT:* Pen or pencil and paper for each player

* *PLAYERS TO KNOW EACH OTHER WELL:* Not necessary

....

THE ORGANIZER CALLS OUT A LETTER OF THE ALPHABET.

The players are asked to write down a two-letter word beginning with that letter. Then under that a three-letter word beginning with the same letter. This does not have to be related in any way to the previous word. Under that a four-letter word.

The winner is the player or pair who gets to the word with the greatest number of letters.

Plurals and different parts of a verb are permitted but proper nouns are not.

Here is how a typical effort might go:

Letter G

GO
GOT
GOOD
GRASP

GATHER
GLIMPSE
GLIMPSED
GRATITUDE
GRATEFULLY
GORGEOUSLY
GENUFLECTING
GRATIFICATION
GENTRIFICATION

Longest word: 14 letters

55 SQUARE DEAL

✳ *NUMBER OF PLAYERS:* Minimum: Six
Maximum: 18

✳ *PLAYED BY INDIVIDUALS*

✳ *ACCOMMODATION:* Enough room for all the players to sit comfortably with somewhere to write

✳ *PREPARATION AND EQUIPMENT:* A pen or pencil and piece of paper for each player; a die

✳ *PLAYERS TO KNOW EACH OTHER WELL:* Not necessary

....

THE PLAYERS ARE EACH ASKED TO DRAW A GRID OF 6 X 6 SQUARES.

They then each roll the die to see who gets the highest score. If two or more tie, they roll again until one has the highest score.

This highest scorer starts by calling out a letter – any letter. He/she and all the other players then write this letter in a square of their choice on their grid. When everyone has written the letter down, the next player on the left calls out another letter. Again, everyone writes this in the square of their choice. The idea is to get as many words as possible across and down (but not diagonally). When every square is full, the players swap their papers for adding up the scores. Each letter used in a word counts as one point.

The winner is the player with the most points.

Score here: 44

B	A	T	H	E	D	BATHED
L	I	E	E	N	E	LIE
O	D	N	A	T	A	AT
T	I	K	V	A	N	VAN
R	W	H	Y	N	O	WHY
Q	U	I	E	T	Z	QUIET

BLOT	AID	TEN	HEAVY	TAN	DEAN

138

56 *HOW GREEN YOU ARE!*

* *NUMBER OF PLAYERS:* Minimum: ten
  Maximum: No limit

* *PLAYED AS A WHOLE GROUP*

* *ACCOMMODATION:* Suited to number of players

* *PREPARATION AND EQUIPMENT:* None

* *PLAYERS TO KNOW EACH OTHER WELL:* Not necessary

....

ONE PLAYER IS SENT OUT OF THE ROOM.

The rest then decide on some action this player must do when they come back into the room, e.g. lie down on the floor, shake hands with a certain person, touch their toes, go to the piano and play something, turn the light off.

The 'audience' sings continuously the words 'How green you are' to the tune of 'Auld Lang Syne'.

They start very softly and, as the participant makes a move towards doing the right thing, they increase the volume. Each time the person does something right they get louder still. If the person looks less likely to achieve it they sing more softly. By the volume of the singing, the player should realize when they are on the right lines. As they are on the point of achieving the objective, the audience sings at full volume. When the player performs the pre-planned action, the audience stops singing and claps.

Another player is then chosen to go out of the room.

57 CHINESE TAKEAWAY

* **NUMBER OF PLAYERS:** Minimum: 12
  Maximum: 50+

* **PLAYED IN TEAMS:** Teams with a minimum of four people and a maximum of eight each

* **ACCOMMODATION:** Room or hall large enough to accommodate the number of teams playing; each team seated round two small tables with a gap of at least 6 feet between each table

* **PREPARATION AND EQUIPMENT:** For each team: one pair of chopsticks and one packet of Jelly Tots or similar small soft sweets

* **PLAYERS TO KNOW EACH OTHER WELL:** Not necessary

....

MEMBERS OF EACH TEAM EMPTY OUT THEIR PACKET OF SWEETS ONTO ONE OF THEIR TWO TABLES.

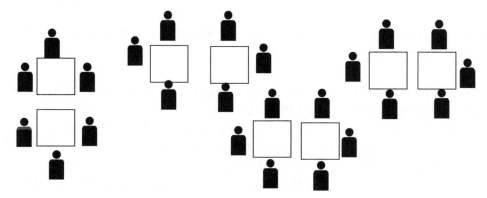

At the word 'Go', each member in turn has to pick up one sweet with the chopsticks and transfer it to the other table.

The first team to have transferred all its sweets is the winner.

FEEDING WITH CHOPSTICKS

* *NUMBER OF PLAYERS:*   Minimum: 20 (two teams of eight+)
    Maximum: No limit – can have as many teams
    as can be accommodated

* *PLAYED IN TEAMS*

* *ACCOMMODATION:* Large room

* *PREPARATION AND EQUIPMENT:* For each team: one small table; one
    shallow dish or bowl filled with small soft sweets, such as Jelly
    Tots; one pair of chopsticks

* *PLAYERS TO KNOW EACH OTHER WELL:* Not necessary

....

THE BOWL OF SWEETS AND THE CHOPSTICKS ARE PLACED ON THE TABLE.

Each team lines up a few feet away from its table.

At the word 'Go' the first two players move forward to their allotted
tables.

The first player picks up the chopsticks and attempts to pick up a
sweet with the chopsticks (using only one hand!) and feed it into
the cupped hands of the second player, who must be standing at
least two feet away and whose hands are up against his/her upper
chest (i.e. not outstretched).

When he/she has succeeded he/she retires and player no. 3 comes
up to the table.

Player no. 2 then tries to feed him/her with a sweet in a similar way.

Player no. 3 then tries to feed player no. 4.

Continue until the last player has been fed a sweet, who then recalls player no. 1, to whom he/she feeds a sweet.

When all the team members have been given a sweet, they call out 'Finish', and the first team to do this is the winner.

59 DRESSING FOR DINNER

* *NUMBER OF PLAYERS:* Any number in teams of 8–12

* *PLAYED IN TEAMS*

* *ACCOMMODATION:* Enough room to accommodate the teams, who need to be able to stand back a little from the tables

* *PREPARATION AND EQUIPMENT:* For each team: a hat, coat and gloves and a small table on which is set out a bar of chocolate (not too thick or chunky) and a knife and fork. Also some wet wipes

* *PLAYERS TO KNOW EACH OTHER WELL:* Not necessary

....

TEAMS LINE UP ALL AT A SIMILAR DISTANCE FROM THEIR RESPECTIVE TABLES, EACH WITH THE HAT, COAT AND GLOVES ON THE FLOOR IMMEDIATELY IN FRONT OF THEM.

At the word 'Go' the first player in each team puts on the hat, coat (buttoning or zipping it up) and gloves. He/she then runs to his/her team's table, picks up the knife and fork and cuts off a small piece of chocolate. He/she eats this, wipes the knife and fork and then runs back to the next member of their team and takes off the items of clothing. This next member puts on the clothing and runs to the table to cut off and eat a piece of chocolate.

The first team whose members all achieve this is the winner. NB: The last player must have taken off the clothing and laid it down before they call out 'Finished'.

60 *TRANSFER WITH A STRAW*

* *NUMBER OF PLAYERS:* Minimum: 12
  Maximum: No limit

* *PLAYED BY TEAMS OF SIX OR MORE PLAYERS*

* *ACCOMMODATION:* Suited to number of players

* *PREPARATION AND EQUIPMENT:* Table for each team; two bowls or dishes, one filled with good quantity of dried peas; one drinking straw for each person

* *PLAYERS TO KNOW EACH OTHER WELL:* Not necessary

....

HAND EVERY PLAYER A DRINKING STRAW.

At the word 'Go' the first person from each team goes to his/her team's table and in the space of one minute tries to transfer as many peas as possible from the full bowl to the empty one by sucking them up with the drinking straw.

At the end of one minute the organizer calls out 'Change' and the next team member comes up to do the same.

When each member has participated, the transferred peas are counted and the winning team is the one that has transferred the most.

61 BEANS IN MUGS

* *NUMBER OF PLAYERS:* Minimum: Ten (i.e. two teams)
  Maximum: No limit

* *PLAYED IN TEAMS OF BETWEEN FIVE AND TEN MEMBERS*

* *ACCOMMODATION:* Large room or hall that can accommodate the number of teams

* *EQUIPMENT NEEDED:* Five mugs for each team; a good supply of kidney beans for each team

....

ON THE FLOOR ABOUT SIX FEET IN FRONT OF EACH TEAM, ARRANGE FIVE MUGS IN THIS SORT OF PATTERN:

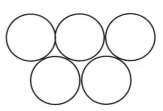

Each team member is given six kidney beans.

When the organizer says 'Go' the first team member starts throwing kidney beans, trying to get as many as possible into one of the cups.

The second team member then comes up and does the same with his/her beans.

When all the team members have had a turn throwing, the beans in their mugs are counted up and the team with the most in the mugs has won.

It helps to have a non-player as a 'picker-up' to retrieve the beans that have not landed in a mug.

62 LINE UP BY BIRTHDAYS

* *NUMBER OF PLAYERS:* Minimum: 20 (two teams of ten+)
  Maximum: No limit

* *PLAYED IN TEAMS*

* *ACCOMMODATION:* Large room

* *PREPARATION AND EQUIPMENT:* None

* *PLAYERS TO KNOW EACH OTHER WELL:* Not necessary

....

ASK THE PLAYERS TO GET THEMSELVES INTO TEAMS OF AT LEAST TEN. IF THE NUMBERS PRESENT MEAN IT IS EASIER TO DIVIDE INTO TEAMS OF, SAY, 12, 13 OR 14, THAT IS FINE.

Each team is asked to stand in a straight line facing the organizer.

At the word 'Go', they are asked to line up in order of their birthdays throughout the year. This sounds simple, but probably will take some time to sort out.

The winning team is the first one to say they have it correct. This should be checked to ensure it is indeed so!

63 *BRING ME*

* *NUMBER OF PLAYERS:* Minimum of ten (i.e. two teams of five)
  Maximum: No limit

* *PLAYED IN TEAMS OF FIVE TO TEN*

* *ACCOMMODATION:* Any size of room or hall that can accommodate the number of teams playing

* *PREPARATION AND EQUIPMENT:* List of objects for the organizer to call out; some of the things can be interpreted in various ways

* *PLAYERS TO KNOW EACH OTHER WELL:* Not necessary

....

THE ORGANIZER STANDS IN THE MIDDLE OF THE ROOM AND CALLS OUT ONE AT A TIME AN OBJECT FROM A LIST HE/SHE HAS COMPILED. THE FIRST TEAM TO GIVE HIM/HER THE OBJECT CALLED WINS A POINT.

Some suggested objects:

1. A lipstick
2. A hair not on anyone's head
3. A hologram
4. A set of teeth not in the owner's mouth (a comb)
5. A paper dart
6. A lash (eyelash pulled out)
7. A nail (fingernail or a DIY nail)
8. A portrait of a head of state (a coin or a stamp)
9. A clip (paper clip, tie clip, etc.)
10. Something to eat
11. A file (nail file or file to contain papers or a Filofax)
12. Lace (shoelace as well as a lace cloth)
13. A ball (could be part of an earring or a ball-point pen)

14. A sock – not on a foot
15. A date (could be a diary or a calendar)
16. A bow (could be a tied shoelace, a hair decoration)
17. A ring
18. A drawing of Noah's ark
19. A fingerprint
20. A brush
21. A top
22. A handkerchief

64 SING THE THING

* NUMBER OF PLAYERS: Minimum: Ten (i.e. two teams)
Maximum: No limit

* PLAYED IN TEAMS OF BETWEEN FIVE AND TEN MEMBERS

* ACCOMMODATION: Suited to number of players

* EQUIPMENT NEEDED: Copy for organizer of list given below

....

THE ORGANIZER CALLS OUT THE FOLLOWING IN TURN:

- A country
- A boy's name
- A US state
- A relative (e.g. mother, brother)
- A season of the year
- An emotion or feeling
- A festival (e.g. Christmas, Easter)
- A girl's name
- A river
- A town
- A tree
- An animal
- A bird
- A flower
- An occupation
- A film

Teams are asked to sing a song containing an example of the category called out. One point for the quickest team. Another point for each team that chooses a song no other team has.

As this game can get quite riotous, it can be helpful to have an assistant to the organizer to act as referee.

65 BACK TO THE NURSERY

* *NUMBER OF PLAYERS:* Minimum: 10
  Maximum: No limit

* *PLAYED IN TEAMS OF FIVE TO TEN*

* *ACCOMMODATION:* Any size of room or hall that can accommodate the number of teams playing

* *PLAYERS TO KNOW EACH OTHER WELL:* Not necessary

....

THE ORGANIZER CALLS OUT A LETTER OF THE ALPHABET. EACH TEAM HAS TO THINK OF A NURSERY RHYME BEGINNING WITH THAT LETTER AND START TO SING IT. THE FIRST TEAM TO DO SO GETS A POINT. THE ORGANIZER THEN CALLS OUT ANOTHER LETTER AND THE TEAMS THINK OF A NURSERY RHYME TO GO WITH THAT.

NB: It would be hard to find a nursery rhyme for some letters, but the following are all possible:

* A
* B
* C
* D
* H

* J
* L
* M
* O
* P

* R
* S
* T
* W

66 NAMES OF RIVERS, PLANTS, ETC.

* **NUMBER OF PLAYERS:** Minimum: Six
  Maximum: No limit

* **PLAYED IN TEAMS OR BY INDIVIDUALS:** Teams of up to six players, or can be played by individuals

* **ACCOMMODATION:** Any size of room or hall that can accommodate the number of teams playing

* **PREPARATION AND EQUIPMENT:** Pen and paper for each team

* **PLAYERS TO KNOW EACH OTHER WELL:** Not necessary

....

THE ORGANIZER CALLS OUT A LETTER OF THE ALPHABET AND EACH TEAM HAS TO WRITE DOWN AN EXAMPLE OF EACH OF THE FOLLOWING BEGINNING WITH THAT LETTER.

1. A boy's name
2. A girl's name
3. A country
4. A city in the UK
5. A city in the USA
6. A city in Europe (not UK)
7. A sportsman or woman (surname)
8. A film star
9. A river
10. A plant
11. An animal
12. A bird

When everyone has done this, each team in turn is asked to call out what it has put down for item 1. Points are scored only when a team has put down something that none of the other teams have.

Then proceed to item 2 and on down the list.

There will probably be a lot of argument about what is acceptable, but the organizer's decision is final!

Examples if letter B were given:

1. A boy's name   *Ben*
2. A girl's name   *Barbara*
3. A country   *Belgium*
4. A city in the UK   *Bradford*
5. A city in the USA   *Boston*
6. A city in Europe (not UK)   *Budapest*
7. A sportsman or woman (surname)   *Seve Ballesteros*
8. A film star (surname)   *Sean Bean*
9. A river   *Blackwater*
10. A plant   *Broccoli*
11. An animal   *Badger*
12. A bird   *Blackbird*

A variation on this theme is to get each team to try to write down, say, a UK city beginning with each of the 26 letters of the alphabet and then similarly award points to those who have something none of the other teams have.

67 PILE 'EM HIGH

* *NUMBER OF PLAYERS:* Minimum: Six
  Maximum: No limit

* *PLAYED AS INDIVIDUALS*

* *ACCOMMODATION:* Suited to number of players

* *PREPARATION AND EQUIPMENT:* A glass bottle (plastic is not suitable, being too lightweight) and two boxes of matches for each group of players

* *PLAYERS TO KNOW EACH OTHER WELL:* Not necessary

....

GET PLAYERS INTO GROUPS OF SIX–TEN. THE GAME IS PLAYED BY INDIVIDUALS WITHIN THE GROUP. IT IS NOT A TEAM GAME.

Each player lays a match across the top of their bottle. The next player adds another match. The next player does the same.

Carry on doing this until some of the matches tip off. The player who made this happen is out and withdraws from the game.

The idea is for each player to place his or her match in a position that will make it difficult for the next player to place a match without tipping some of the matches off.

Finally, just one player remains who has not caused any matches to tip off.

If there has been more than one group playing the game, all the winners can then compete together to get an overall winner. If there were only two or three groups, include the runners-up in the final.

68 DRAW IT OUT

* *NUMBER OF PLAYERS:* Minimum: Ten (i.e. two teams of five)
  Maximum: No limit

* *PLAYED IN TEAMS OF FIVE TO TEN*

* *ACCOMMODATION:* Any size room or hall that can accommodate the number of teams playing

* *PREPARATION AND EQUIPMENT:* For the organizer: list of things to be drawn; for each team: a pen or pencil and lots of paper

* *PLAYERS TO KNOW EACH OTHER WELL:* Not necessary

....

THE ORGANIZER ASKS FOR ONE MEMBER OF EACH TEAM TO COME UP AND HE/SHE WHISPERS TO THEM ALL SOMETHING THEY ARE TO DRAW.

They return to their teams to draw this and the other members have to guess what it is. No writing is permitted and no speaking is allowed other than 'Yes' or 'No' as people try to guess what has been drawn.

When someone guesses correctly he/she goes up to the organizer, whispers the answer and is given something else to draw. He/she goes back to his team and draws this.

When a team has guessed everything on the organizer's list, he calls out 'Finish' and announces the winning team.

Suggested lists

General	Biblical	Films
An eagle	Noah's ark	*The Ladykillers*
A castle	Goliath	*Bambi*
A tractor	Feeding the 5,000	*Gone with the Wind*
A beefburger	Paul being shipwrecked	*The Deer Hunter*
The planets	Jonah and the whale	*Star Wars*
A pineapple	The walls of Jericho	*Hook*
A boxing match	Walking on water	*Treasure Island*
An oasis	The Ten Commandments	*Dead Poets Society*
Christmas	Gold, frankincense and myrrh	*On Golden Pond*
A barbecue	Stilling the storm	*The Gold Rush*
A chef	Ruth gleaning	*The Third Man*
A lion	Turning the water into wine	*101 Dalmatians*
A cowboy	Joseph's coat of many colours	*The Sound of Music*
A doctor	Samson	*High Noon*
An Easter egg	Cain and Abel	*Narnia*
A birthday cake	Shepherds watching their flocks	*South Pacific*
A dragon	Jacob's ladder	*Titanic*
Italy	The seven churches of Asia	*The Lion King*

Other suggestions for lists might be:

- Books
- Trades or occupations
- Famous people

(69) DO IT IN MIME

* *NUMBER OF PLAYERS:* Minimum: Ten (i.e. two teams of five)
   Maximum: No limit

* *PLAYED IN TEAMS OF FIVE TO TEN*

* *ACCOMMODATION:* Any size of room or hall that can accommodate the number of teams playing

* *PREPARATION AND EQUIPMENT:* For the organizer: list of topics to be acted

* *PLAYERS TO KNOW EACH OTHER WELL:* Not necessary

....

THE ORGANIZER ANNOUNCES THE CATEGORY OF TOPICS FOR MIMING, E.G. FILMS, OCCUPATIONS, ETC. HE/SHE THEN ASKS FOR ONE MEMBER OF EACH TEAM TO COME UP AND WHISPERS TO THEM ALL SOMETHING THEY ARE TO MIME.

They return to their teams to mime this and the other members have to guess what it is. Before starting they can each hold up the number of fingers to show the number of words in what they will be miming. No speaking is allowed other than 'Yes' or 'No' as people try to guess what is being mimed

When someone guesses correctly he goes up to the organizer, whispers the answer and is given something else to mime. He/she goes back to his/her team and mimes this.

When a team has guessed everything on the organizer's list, he/she calls out 'finish' and announces the winning team.

Suggested lists — but you will probably be able to think of others

Occupation	Famous people	Films
Blacksmith	King Alfred	*Singing in the Rain*
Nurse	Samson	*Oliver Twist*
Chef	Robin Hood	*Gone with the Wind*
Racing driver	Buffalo Bill	*Dumbo*
Hairdresser	Maria von Trapp	*The Gold Rush*
Astronomer	Frank Bruno (or other boxer)	*Driving Miss Daisy*
Call-centre operator	Gandhi	*Treasure Island*
Milkmaid	Pocahontas	*Dead Poets Society*
Boxer	Johnny Appleseed	*On Golden Pond*
Postman	Delia Smith (or other (well-known cook)	*The Big Sleep*
Athlete	Christopher Columbus	*The Third Man*
Potter	Neil Armstrong	*Giant*
Doctor	Van Gogh	*The Sound of Music*
Supermarket checkout operator	Ivan the Terrible	*The Dirty Dozen*
Window cleaner	Isaac Newton	*Three Men in a Boat*
Photographer	Horatio Nelson	*Four Weddings and a Funeral*

70 SAY IT WITH NUMBERS

* *NUMBER OF PLAYERS:* Minimum: 20 (i.e. two teams of ten)
  Maximum: No limit

* *PLAYED IN TEAMS OF TEN* (but can be adapted to smaller teams)

* *ACCOMMODATION:* Any size of room or hall that can accommodate the number of teams playing

* *PREPARATION AND EQUIPMENT:* List of questions for the organizer to call out; two sets of ten cards for each team. In large writing on each should be one of the numbers between 0 and 9, inclusive

* *PLAYERS TO KNOW EACH OTHER WELL:* Not necessary

....

EACH MEMBER OF EACH TEAM IS GIVEN TWO NUMBERED CARDS. IF TEAMS HAVE FEWER THAN TEN MEMBERS, SOME MEMBERS WILL NEED TO HAVE THREE CARDS.

The organizer asks the questions on his list. The team whose members stand up showing the numbers in the correct order wins a point.

Examples of possible questions:

1. When was the Battle of Hastings? – 1066
2. What year was D-Day? – 1944
3. What is a gross? – 144
4. 96 plus 9 plus 30? – 135
5. How many yards in a mile? 1,760
6. When did Columbus discover the New World? – 1492
7. When was the American Declaration of Independence? –1776
8. When was the Battle of the Somme? – 1916
9. In what year did the *Titanic* sink? – 1912

10. How many Psalms are there? – 150
11. When was the Russian Revolution? – 1917
12. Days in a leap year? – 366
13. Pearl Harbour? – 1942
14. Wall Street Crash? –1929
15. A millennium plus a decade? – 1010
16. How many trombones in the big parade? – 76
17. How many letters in the alphabet? – 26
18. How many Arabian Nights? – 1,001

71 TEAR 'EM OFF A STRIP

* **NUMBER OF PLAYERS:** Minimum: Six
  Maximum: No limit

* **PLAYED AS INDIVIDUALS**

* **ACCOMMODATION:** Suited to number of players

* **PREPARATION AND EQUIPMENT:** One double-spread page of a broadsheet newspaper for each person. A couple of wet wipes to hand round at the end of the game

* **PLAYERS TO KNOW EACH OTHER:** Not necessary

....

THE AIM OF THIS GAME IS TO SEE WHICH PLAYER CAN TEAR OFF THE LONGEST CONTINUOUS STRIP OF NEWSPAPER. THEY ARE TOLD THEY WILL BE GIVEN FOUR MINUTES TO DO THIS.

At the word 'Go', they all start.

When the four minutes are up, they players are asked to stop and the strips are measured against each other to find the winner.

Newsprint tends to come off on the hands, so when the game is over you might like to hand round a couple of wet wipes for players to clean themselves up.

72 CLUMPS

* NUMBER OF PLAYERS: Minimum: 25
                     Maximum: No limit

* PLAYED IN TEAMS OR BY INDIVIDUALS: Individuals

* ACCOMMODATION: Large room or hall

* PREPARATION AND EQUIPMENT: Background music able to be turned on and off easily. Or a good pianist or keyboard player

* PLAYERS TO KNOW EACH OTHER WELL: Not necessary

....

MUSIC STARTS. THE PLAYERS WANDER ABOUT THE ROOM UNTIL THE MUSIC STOPS. THE ORGANIZER THEN CALLS OUT 'GET INTO...', AND A NUMBER.

The players then have to get into small groups of the number given. Almost always there will one or more players left over, who are then out and go and sit down.

The game goes on until there is only one player left.

As the number of players remaining gets smaller, the organizer will need to call out smaller numbers, until there are only three players left.

He/she will then call out 'Get into twos' and one player will be left out. The remaining two are joint winners.

73 BIGAMY

* *NUMBER OF PLAYERS:* Over 20 and preferably more

* *PLAYED BY TRIOS*

* *ACCOMMODATION:* Large room or hall

* *PREPARATION AND EQUIPMENT:* An upright chair for all taking part in the game; a CD player, tape or pianist

* *PLAYERS TO KNOW EACH OTHER WELL:* Not necessary

....

THE CHAIRS ARE SET OUT IN THREES SIDE BY SIDE RANDOMLY AROUND THE ROOM, THOUGH GENERALLY FACING INWARDS. THIS COULD BE A TYPICAL PATTERN, BUT WHAT IS IMPORTANT IS THAT THE OCCUPANT OF EACH CHAIR CAN SEE AT LEAST SOME OF THE OTHER PLAYERS.

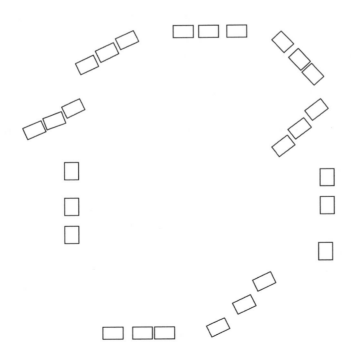

Each trio of chairs is occupied by one man in the centre with a lady either side (his 'bigamous wives'), with the exception of one set of chairs, where the man has only one wife. When the music starts he gets up with his 'wife', goes to another set of chairs and steals a 'wife' from there, returning to his own chair. The man left with one wife short has to go to another set of chairs and do the same. When the music stops the last man to have acquired a second 'wife' is out, together with his two wives. He takes away his three chairs and retires to the side of the room.

When the music restarts, the man with only one 'wife' gets up to steal another.

In this way the number of trios is whittled down until there is only one man and one 'wife' left.

It would be good to think of an appropriate prize for the man, such as a cheap and gaudy ring – the sort that is sometimes found in Christmas crackers.

74 *I PASS THESE SCISSORS ...*

* *NUMBER OF PLAYERS:* Minimum: Six
  Maximum: 20

* *PLAYED BY INDIVIDUALS*

* *ACCOMMODATION:* Room or hall in which all players can be seated on chairs or stools in a circle

* *PREPARATION AND EQUIPMENT:* A large pair of scissors

* *PLAYERS TO KNOW EACH OTHER WELL:* Not necessary

The organizer hands the scissors to the person on his/her right, saying either 'I pass these scissors crossed' or 'I pass these scissors uncrossed', and invites that person to pass the scissors on to his/her right-hand neighbour in exactly the same way. If the organizer judges the scissors to have been passed correctly, he/she will ask the person to repeat the action and then if he/she is satisfied, welcome that person as a fellow conspirator. As the scissors are passed round the circle, those in the know will handle them in different ways, i.e. holding them by the blades, by the handles, open, closed, upside down, etc. The idea is to see how many people one can get 'in the know' within a suggested time limit of ten minutes. The secret is not in the scissors at all, but whether the person passing them on sits with legs crossed or uncrossed.

NB: It is important to emphasize that, when a player guesses the secret, he/she doesn't call out the answer, but continues in the game, passing the scissors correctly.

75 MY AUNT HETTY

* **NUMBER OF PLAYERS:** Minimum: Six
  Maximum: 20

* **PLAYED BY INDIVIDUALS**

* **ACCOMMODATION:** Room or hall in which the organizer and all players can be seated on chairs or stools in a circle

* **PREPARATION AND EQUIPMENT:** None

* **PLAYERS TO KNOW EACH OTHER WELL:** Not necessary

....

PLAYERS SHOULD BE SEATED IN A CIRCLE. THE ORGANIZER STARTS BY MAKING A STATEMENT ALONG THE FOLLOWING LINES:

* 'My Aunt Hetty likes coffee, but she doesn't like tea.'
* 'Aunt Hetty likes tennis, but doesn't care for golf.'
* 'She likes holidays in Cornwall, but dislikes Devon.'

It will be seen that everything she likes contains a double letter, whereas everything she dislikes has no double letters.

Going round the circle, each person makes a statement concerning Aunt Hetty's likes and dislikes. Sometimes people will guess quite soon what constitutes these likes or dislikes. Sometimes they will hit upon it by accident, not knowing quite why. When someone is right, the organizer tells him he/she is right, but does not reveal why. It is important that none of the competitors say what they think the secret is, but simply make statements so that the organizer can see whether they are right.

The game goes on either until everyone has guessed or until people are tired of it.

76 ASSOCIATION OF IDEAS

* NUMBER OF PLAYERS: Minimum: six
                     Maximum: 20

* PLAYED BY INDIVIDUALS

* ACCOMMODATION: Room or hall in which all players can be seated on
     chairs or stools in a circle

* PREPARATION AND EQUIPMENT: None

* PLAYERS TO KNOW EACH OTHER WELL: Not necessary

....

SEATED IN A CIRCLE, THE PLAYERS ALL CLAP TOGETHER THREE TIMES.

The organizer starts off the clapping to get the rhythm going and
then after a phrase of claps calls out a word. As soon as he/she has
done so, everyone claps three times again and the player on his/her
left must call out a word he/she associates with it.

The clapping resumes and the next person on the left must call out
a word he/she associates with the one just called.

As an example:

Clap, clap, clap
Sea
Clap, clap, clap
Blue
Clap, clap, clap
Moon
Clap, clap, clap
Rocket

Clap, clap, clap
Fireworks, etc.

Or:

Clap, clap, clap
Mouse
Clap, clap, clap
Cheese
Clap, clap, clap
Toast
Clap, clap, clap
Burnt
Clap, clap, clap
Offering

If anyone breaks the rhythm by not saying a word quickly enough, he/she is out and must move their chair away or sit with their arms folded.

Any player can challenge the word, saying he/she can't see the association. The game continues until one person only remains – the winner.

77 THE LAST SHALL BE FIRST

* **NUMBER OF PLAYERS:** Minimum: Six
  Maximum: 25

* **PLAYED BY INDIVIDUALS**

* **ACCOMMODATION:** Room or hall in which all players can be seated on
  chairs or stools in a circle

* **PREPARATION AND EQUIPMENT:** None

* **PLAYERS TO KNOW EACH OTHER WELL:** Not necessary

....

*THE PLAYERS ALL SIT IN THE CIRCLE AND THE ORGANIZER STARTS OFF BY SAYING THE
NAME OF A TOWN OR CITY. THE NEXT PERSON ON HIS/HER LEFT THEN HAS TO SAY
ANOTHER TOWN OR CITY BEGINNING WITH THE LAST LETTER OF THE PREVIOUS ONE.*

It then passes on round the circle in the same manner.

The other players can challenge anyone they feel hesitates too
much, repeats a name that has already been used or gives a name
they think may not exist.
If the majority agree to the challenge, that player is out and either
moves back from the circle or sits with arms folded.

The last player in is the winner.

Examples:

* *London, Newcastle, Epsom, Manchester, Ripon*
* *Dallas, San Diego, Omaha, Atlanta*

Or the cities need not all be in one country:

- *Richmond, Detroit, Tulsa, Auckland, Durham, Moscow, Washington, Newark, Kathmandu*

78 KEEP TALKING

* **NUMBER OF PLAYERS:** Minimum: Six
  Maximum: 12–16

* **PLAYED BY INDIVIDUALS**

* **ACCOMMODATION:** Suited to the number of players

* **PREPARATION AND EQUIPMENT:** A list of topics on which players will be asked to speak; a watch or clock with a second hand or a timer that can be set to one minute

* **PLAYERS TO KNOW EACH OTHER WELL:** Not necessary

....

THE PLAYERS IN TURN ARE GIVEN A TOPIC, ON WHICH THEY ARE ASKED TO SPEAK FOR ONE MINUTE.

At the word 'Go', the organizer notes the time on the watch or clock and the player starts to speak on his/her given topic.

As he/she is speaking, any other player can interrupt if they feel he/she has deviated from the subject, hesitated too much or repeated him/herself. The organizer acts as referee and decides whether the interruption is justified. If the speaker survives the whole minute, he/she gets a point.

After each player has had a turn a second round can be played between the players who got a point.

A third or subsequent round can be played to determine an overall winner.

Possible topics:

- Winter sports
- Christmas dinner
- My pet hate
- Wildlife in Africa
- Barbecues
- Keeping a diary
- Map reading
- Bad habits
- Parties
- Abstract art
- The Wild West
- Fireworks

79 NEVER SAY YES OR NO

* *NUMBER OF PLAYERS:* Minimum: Eight
  Maximum 20

* *PLAYED BY INDIVIDUALS*

* *ACCOMMODATION:* Room or hall in which all players can be seated on chairs or stools in a circle

* *PREPARATION AND EQUIPMENT:* The organizer will need to think of a number of questions to ask the participants – ones to which the most obvious answer is 'yes' or 'no'.

* *PLAYERS TO KNOW EACH OTHER WELL:* Not necessary

....

THE ORGANIZER SHOOTS QUICK-FIRE QUESTIONS AT PLAYERS TO WHICH THE MOST OBVIOUS ANSWERS ARE EITHER 'YES' OR 'NO'. HOWEVER, ANY PLAYER WHO ANSWERS WITH EITHER OF THESE WORDS IS OUT AND MUST EITHER WITHDRAW FROM THE CIRCLE OR SIT WITH HIS/HER ARMS FOLDED. THE PLAYERS ARE NOT QUESTIONED IN ANY ORDER AND ANY ONE OF THEM MAY GET SEVERAL QUESTIONS IN A ROW. THE ORGANIZER MAY DECREE THAT ANY PLAYER WHO HESITATES UNDULY IS ALSO OUT.

Sometimes this is played with everyone having two or three 'lives' so they are not out the first time they make a mistake.

Typical questions might include:

* Do you like Indian food?
* Have you ever travelled to the East?
* Do you play golf?
* Do you know most of the people here?
* Are you very competitive?
* Have you been away this year?

- Abroad?
- Weather good?
- Is your birthday in winter or summer? Did you say summer?
- Do you find this sort of thing stressful?
- Do you think he should have been out?
- Do you watch a lot of television?
- Are you a keen reader?
- Do you like fiction best?
- Or biographies?

80 NOT THAT WORD!

* *NUMBER OF PLAYERS:* Minimum: Six
                       Maximum:12–16

* *PLAYED BY INDIVIDUALS*

* *ACCOMMODATION:* Suited to number of players

* *PREPARATION AND EQUIPMENT:* A number of cards or slips of paper on each of which is written the topic to be spoken about and three other very obvious words connected with the topic

* *PLAYERS TO KNOW EACH OTHER WELL:* Not necessary, but sometimes more fun if they do

....

THE FIRST PLAYER TAKES A CARD AND IS TOLD HE/SHE MUST SPEAK ON THE TOPIC ON THE CARD FOR ONE MINUTE WITHOUT BRINGING IN ANY OF THE OTHER WORDS. IF HE/ SHE SURVIVES THE MINUTE HE/SHE GETS A POINT.

The players in turn each take a card, announce what the words on it are and start to speak on the subject on their card.

When everyone has had a go, you can play a second round between the players who have won a point.

Those who win a point in this round go on to a third round.

Do this until there is a clear winner.

Suggestions for the cards:

• Measles – illness, rash, infectious
• Twins – two, children, identical

- Tyrol – Austria, mountains(s), Alps
- Space exploration – rocket, moon, astronaut
- D-Day – war, invasion, Normandy
- Bed – sleep, lie, night
- The Ten Commandments – Moses, Israelites, God
- Doctor – sick, well, medicine
- Tiger – cat, wild, stripes
- Teacher – school, children, learn
- Christmas – celebrate, birth, Bethlehem
- Hymns – God, sing, praise
- Rain – wet, fall, water
- Jamaica – island, Caribbean, West Indies
- Gossip – talk, rumours, spread
- Ark – Noah, animals, flood
- Chopsticks – Chinese, eat, hold
- Infinity – limitless, eternity, distance
- Pirate – sea, skull and crossbones, ship
- Milk – white, drink, cow
- St Bernard – dog, rescue, Alps
- Surf – ocean, wave, wind
- Alligator – reptile, crocodile, water
- Weather – rain, sun, wind

81 EXCLUSIVELY MINE

* *NUMBER OF PLAYERS:* Minimum: Four
  Maximum: 16

* *PLAYED BY INDIVIDUALS*

* *ACCOMMODATION:* Any size room in which the players can sit and hear each other well

* *PREPARATION AND EQUIPMENT:*
  Pen or pencil and paper for each player
  Timer or watch for the organizer

* *PLAYERS TO KNOW EACH OTHER WELL:* Not necessary

....

THE ORGANIZER ANNOUNCES A CATEGORY AND A LETTER OF THE ALPHABET.

Suggested categories:

* Occupations
* Books or films
* Items found in pocket or handbag
* Famous person (Christian name or surname)
* Hobby or sport
* Something to eat
* A song
* An animal

The players then have five minutes to write down all the words they can think of beginning with that letter in the category decided.

When the time is up, the players in turn read out what they have written down. If any other players have the same word, they say so and they have to cross it out.

When everyone has read out their list, the players count up their scores, with one point for each word no one else has got.

Probably about four rounds are right for this game. At the end everyone adds up their grand total to find the overall winner.

82 READING IN A CROWDED TRAIN

* NUMBER OF PLAYERS: Minimum: Six
                     Maximum: 16

* PLAYED BY INDIVIDUALS

* ACCOMMODATION: Any size of room in which the players can be seated on upright chairs in two rows facing each other

* PREPARATION AND EQUIPMENT: One broadsheet newspaper for each player. These need not be the same editions, but do need to have the same number of pages; a few wet wipes

* PLAYERS TO KNOW EACH OTHER WELL: Not necessary

....

THE CHAIRS ARE SET OUT IN TWO ROWS FACING EACH OTHER, WITH NO GAPS BETWEEN CHAIRS. THE PLAYERS THEN SIT DOWN. THEY SHOULD BE AS CLOSE TO THE OPPOSITE ROW AS POSSIBLE, I.E. KNEES TOUCHING.

They are then each given a copy of a newspaper whose pages have all been mixed up. At the word 'Go' each player has to sort his/her paper into the right order. This is quite difficult as the players are seated in such close proximity.

The first person to have his/her paper sorted out calls out 'finished' and is the winner.

Newsprint tends to come off on the hands, so when the game is over you might like to hand round a few wet wipes for players to clean themselves up.

83 THE ONE THAT DIDN'T GET AWAY

* NUMBER OF PLAYERS: Minimum: 16
  Maximum: 40

* PLAYED BY INDIVIDUALS

* ACCOMMODATION: Large room or hall. Or it can be played outdoors

* PREPARATION AND EQUIPMENT: For each player, two pieces of paper cut out in the shape of a fish. Threaded through the head end should be a piece of wool long enough to tie the fish round a person's ankle so that it trails on the ground

* PLAYERS TO KNOW EACH OTHER WELL: Not necessary

....

WHEN ALL THE PLAYERS HAVE THEIR TWO FISH TIED ROUND THEIR ANKLES, AT THE WORD 'GO' THEY MOVE ROUND THE ROOM TRYING TO TREAD ON OTHER PLAYERS' FISH. THIS WILL TEAR THE FISH AND DETACH THEM FROM THE ANKLE.

The aim is for each player to tear away the fish of as many other players as possible without getting his/her own torn away. When a player has lost both his/her fish, he/she should retire to the side of the room. The last player with one or two fish still intact is the winner.

84 SPOT YOUR HUSBAND BY HIS FEET

* *NUMBER OF PLAYERS:* Minimum: Five married couples
with others present (couples and/or singles) as
an audience
Maximum: Eight married couples

* *PLAYED IN TEAMS OR BY INDIVIDUALS:* Married couples, plus audience

* *ACCOMMODATION:* Room or hall in which at least five men can lie full-
length on the floor and the audience has a good view of them

* *PREPARATION AND EQUIPMENT:* A sheet or blanket large enough to
cover the husband of each couple participating

* *PLAYERS TO KNOW EACH OTHER WELL:* Not necessary, but it is more fun if
they do

....

PICK OUT FIVE MARRIED COUPLES IN WHICH THE MEN ARE OF FAIRLY SIMILAR HEIGHT.

The wives are sent out of the room and while they are away the
husbands lie down on the floor, where each is covered with a
blanket or sheet with just his feet remaining visible.

The wives are brought in one at a time and they are asked to
undertake a test that will indicate the closeness of their married
relationship. They are then invited to identify their husbands by
their feet.

The process usually produces a lot of laughs, and at the end the
couples are divided into 'successes' and 'failures'.

180

85 DESCRIBE WHOM YOU WERE WITH

* **NUMBER OF PLAYERS:** Between nine and about 24

* **PLAYED BY INDIVIDUALS**

* **ACCOMMODATION:** Suited to number of players

* **EQUIPMENT NEEDED:** Pens or pencils and sheets of paper

* **PLAYERS TO KNOW EACH OTHER WELL:** Not necessary

....

ASK PLAYERS TO GET INTO GROUPS OF THREE, WITH NO HUSBANDS AND WIVES IN THE SAME GROUP. GIVE THEM FIVE MINUTES TO CHAT GENERALLY TOGETHER. TRY TO AVOID HAVING ALL MEN OR ALL WOMEN IN ANY GROUP.

Then ask one person from each group (a man if possible) to go out of the room. While outside, he is then given a pen and paper and asked to describe the two people he has been talking to for the past five minutes, e.g. the colour and style of their hair, what they are wearing, etc.

They then come back into the room and read out what they have written. When compared with whom they are describing, what they say will probably be found to be both inaccurate and amusing.

86 CAPTION THE PICTURE

* **NUMBER OF PLAYERS:** Minimum: Ten
                        Maximum: 25

* **PLAYED BY INDIVIDUALS**

* **ACCOMMODATION:** Suited to number of players

* **PREPARATION AND EQUIPMENT:** Photos of people present, in what could be interpreted as unusual or amusing situations or poses. These should be mounted on larger sheets of paper with room underneath to write the captions. A pen for each player

  Example of photos we have used have been people doing the following: sitting in the stocks, tucking into an outsized helping of gateau, looking disapprovingly at others eating outsized helpings of gateau, bouncing on a trampoline, relaxing on four-poster bed, feeding a donkey, and, of course, pulling funny faces.

* **PLAYERS TO KNOW EACH OTHER WELL:** Necessary

....

THE PHOTOS CAN EITHER BE STUCK ON THE WALL OR, IN A SMALLER GATHERING, PASSED ROUND TO INDIVIDUAL PLAYERS.

Players are invited to write an amusing caption under each picture.

When this has been done, the players are invited to put a tick against what they feel is the wittiest caption for each picture. These are read out to all present and the authors asked to identify themselves.

87 PICTURES FROM A SQUIGGLE

✻ *NUMBER OF PLAYERS:* Minimum: Six
Maximum: 20

✻ *PLAYED BY INDIVIDUALS*

✻ *ACCOMMODATION:* Room or hall in which all players can be seated and be comfortable enough to draw

✻ *PREPARATION AND EQUIPMENT:* For each player, a pen or pencil and a numbered photocopied sheet of a squiggle, each person having the same squiggle

✻ *PLAYERS TO KNOW EACH OTHER WELL:* Not necessary

....

PLAYERS ARE ASKED TO TURN THE SQUIGGLE INTO A PICTURE.

When they have done this, the pictures are passed round or fixed to the wall and players place a tick against the one they think the best and so a winner is determined.

Some suggested squiggles – or, of course, you can make up your own:

WHOSE PORTRAIT?

* *NUMBER OF PLAYERS:* Minimum: Six
  Maximum: 20

* *PLAYED BY INDIVIDUALS*

* *ACCOMMODATION:* Room or hall in which all players can be seated on chairs or stools in a circle and in which they can see most of the other players

* *PREPARATION AND EQUIPMENT:* For each player a pen or pencil and a sheet of paper (about A5 size) numbered in top right-hand corner; a hat, bag or box of slips of paper, each one containing the name of one of the players; another sheet of paper for each player

* *PLAYERS TO KNOW EACH OTHER WELL:* Preferable

....

EACH PLAYER DRAWS A SLIP OF PAPER FROM THE HAT.

They are given five minutes to draw a portrait of the person whose name appears on the slip. While doing this they should try not to be seen looking at the person they are drawing. If they cannot easily see the person they are to draw, they can ask to swap their seat with someone else.

After five minutes the portraits are collected and either laid out in the centre of the room or passed round the room to all the players.

The players then have to guess who the subject of each numbered portrait is, and write down his or her name against the appropriate number on their sheets of paper.

The winner is the one with the most correct guesses.

 **LIMERICKS**

* *NUMBER OF PLAYERS:* Minimum: Eight
  Maximum: No limit

* *PLAYED BY INDIVIDUALS, PAIRS OR SMALL GROUPS*

* *ACCOMMODATION:* Suited to number of players

* *PREPARATION AND EQUIPMENT:* A pen and pencil for each group, pair or individual player and sheet of paper with a printed sample limerick; also on the paper four names – people or places

* *PLAYERS TO KNOW EACH OTHER WELL:* Not necessary

....

RECITE THE SAMPLE LIMERICK A COUPLE OF TIMES TO HELP THE PLAYERS TO RECOGNIZE THE RHYTHM.

Then tell them they are to compose their own limericks, incorporating any two of the names they have been given on the sheet of paper.

Give them ten minutes to do this. If requested, you can extend this time to 15 minutes.

Suggested names: Bill, Jane, Sally, Pete, Phil, Ray, Steve, John, Jack, Milly
(easy to rhyme with) France, Leeds, Brazil, Chile, Rome, Wales, Spain, Bonn

Sample limerick:

There was a young lady from Hyde,
Who ate a green apple and died.
The apple fermented,
Inside the lamented,
And made cider inside her inside.

90 UPDATE YOUR NURSERY RHYMES

* NUMBER OF PLAYERS: Minimum: Six
                     Maximum: No limit

* PLAYED BY INDIVIDUALS, PAIRS OR SMALL GROUPS

* ACCOMMODATION: Any size of room in which the groups can be accommodated

* PREPARATION AND EQUIPMENT: A pen or pencil and paper and a photocopy of the sheet below for each person, pair or group

* PLAYERS TO KNOW EACH OTHER WELL: Not necessary

....

MUCH OF THE WORDING AND MANY OF THE SENTIMENTS OF WELL-LOVED NURSERY RHYMES WOULD BE FROWNED ON BY THE HEALTH AND SAFETY AUTHORITIES AND POLITICAL-CORRECTNESS GURUS OF TODAY. SO TRY REWRITING SOME OF THE WELL-KNOWN ONES.

See what you can do with some of the rhymes below. They needn't rhyme or scan and extra lines may be added if you wish. You don't have to attempt all of them. When you have finished, choose one of your group to read them out when asked.

—————————

Little Miss Muffet sat on her tuffet
Eating her curds and whey.
Along came a spider
And sat down beside her
And frightened Miss Muffet away.

Little Boy Blue, come blow your horn;
The sheep's in the meadow; the cow's in the corn.
But where's the boy who looks after the sheep?
He's under a haystack fast asleep.

――――――――――

'Where are you going to, my pretty maid?'
'I'm going a milking, sir,' she said.
'What is your fortune, my pretty maid?'
'My face is my fortune, sir' she said.

――――――――――

Jack Spratt could eat no fat;
His wife could eat no lean.
And so betwixt the two of them
They licked the platter clean.

――――――――――

'Baa, baa, black sheep, have you any wool?'
'Yes sir, yes sir, three bags full.
One for the master and one for the dame
And one for the little boy who lives down the lane.'

――――――――――

Three blind mice, three blind mice,
See how they run, see how they run.
They all ran after the farmer's wife,
Who cut off their tails with a carving knife;
Did ever you see such a thing in your life
As three blind mice?

――――――――――

There was an old woman who lived in a shoe.
She had so many children,
She didn't know what to do.
She gave them some broth
Without any bread,
And whipped them all soundly
And sent them to bed.

To give you the idea of how it can work, here are two examples:

_____

Little Jack Horner
Sat in the corner (as he lived in a bungalow, there was no 'naughty
*   step' for him)*
Eating his low-fat, low-sugar Christmas pie.
He put in his thumb (having first cleaned it thoroughly with an
*   antiseptic wipe)*
And pulled out a plum,
And, having had installed in him a sense of his own self-worth, said
*   'What a good boy am I'.*

_____

Humpty Dumpty sat on the wall – even though such an activity was
*   expressly forbidden by the local Health and Safety Committee.*
Humpty Dumpty had a great fall, which might well have been
*   predicted.*

All the king's horses and all the king's men (well, just a few of them, as
*   numbers*
had been greatly reduced by defence spending cuts and most of the
*   others were serving in Iraq or Afghanistan)*
Couldn't put Humpty together again
As the local A & E had been closed and the nearest was now 45 miles
*   away.*
There was nothing to be done except for Mother Dumpty to mourn her
*   son*
and prepare to sue the owners of the wall.

91 THAT'S A FUNNY ANSWER!

✳ *NUMBER OF PLAYERS:* Minimum: Eight
Maximum: 20

✳ *PLAYED BY INDIVIDUALS:* A non-competitive game for individuals

✳ *ACCOMMODATION:* Enough room for all present to sit in a rough circle

✳ *PREPARATION AND EQUIPMENT:* 60 cards with questions and answers
printed on them

✳ *PLAYERS TO KNOW EACH OTHER WELL:* Not necessary, but it is more fun if
they do

....

*GET 60 CARDS. ON 30 OF THEM WRITE THE QUESTIONS BELOW, AND ON THE OTHER 30
WRITE THE ANSWERS BELOW.*

Gather the group into a circle. Hold the cards with the questions
like a fan in one hand and the cards with the answers in the other.
Ask the first player to choose someone to answer his/her question
(i.e. the second player). The first player then draws a question and
the second player draws an answer. The first player reads his/her
card aloud. Then the second player reads his/her answer aloud.
The cards are then discarded. The game goes on either until all the
questions are asked and answered or until you feel the players have
got tired of it.

Some suggested questions

• Would you like to be a millionaire?
• Would you like to find yourself in a harem?
• Do you enjoy parties?
• Do you often eat in Chinese restaurants?

- Do you enjoy going to work?
- Do you like Indian food?
- Do you wear a wig?
- Have you any shortcomings?
- Do you like jazz?
- Are you always as polite as today?
- Have you ever walked in your sleep?
- Do you snore?
- Do you try to keep fit?
- Would you like to sit next to me?
- Do you like children?
- Can you touch your nose with your tongue?
- Are you often late for appointments?
- Have you any pets?
- Have you ever been convicted of speeding?
- Are you jealous?
- Do you always eat so much?
- Do you regularly oversleep?
- Have you ever fallen asleep during the sermon?
- Do you usually send Valentine cards?
- Are you modest?
- Would you like to have many new friends?
- Do you often tell lies?
- Can you flatter?
- Can I rely on you?

Some suggested answers

- *I'll think about it later.*
- *It would do no harm.*
- *Towards evening when I'm feeling amorous.*
- *While in a poetic mood.*
- *Only at Christmas.*
- *If it's cold outdoors.*
- *No, no, no, no!*
- *Yes, on payday.*
- *Probably half a dozen times a year.*
- *Yes, but never on a Sunday.*

- *To while away the time.*
- *Only while having a bath.*
- *Only while having a rest at a health resort.*
- *No, it makes me ill.*
- *This is my hobby.*
- *When I am on the verge of despair, yes.*
- *It is my life's work.*
- *I do it with the greatest pleasure.*
- *Once, but only in a weak moment.*
- *I'm not capable of such a stupid thing.*
- *No, I'm well-bred.*
- *I'll answer you in private.*
- *I sometimes pretend to.*
- *Only in the bathroom.*
- *Every other day.*
- *By no means.*

92 BALLOON DEBATE

* NUMBER OF PLAYERS: Minimum: 12
                     Maximum: No limit

* PLAYED BY THE GROUP AS A WHOLE

* ACCOMMODATION: Any size of room or hall that can accommodate
    the 'debaters' and their audience

* PREPARATION AND EQUIPMENT: Four or five chairs for 'debaters',
    placed facing everyone else; four or five people will have been
    approached in advance and told the part they will play

* PLAYERS TO KNOW EACH OTHER WELL: Not necessary

....

EACH OF THE DEBATERS IS GIVEN A PART TO PLAY. THESE CAN BE EITHER SERIOUS,
SUCH AS DOCTOR, FARMER, ENGINEER, AIRPORT CONTROLLER, BUILDER...

...or rather flippant, such as cosmetic surgeon, pet beautician,
agony aunt, writer of birthday-card rhymes, sports personality.

Another idea is 'ones we love to hate', e.g. traffic warden, property
developer, second-hand-car salesman, tax collector, etc.

The audience is told that the players are up in a balloon, which is in
trouble. To keep it in the air and enable it to make a safe landing,
all but one of the occupants must be ejected. Each one must give
a short speech justifying why he or she should be the one saved by
remaining in the balloon.

After each person has spoken, the debate is thrown open to
questions from the audience.

Finally, a vote is taken on who should be saved.

As an additional feature, the winner can be given the emergency rations to eat. These will consist of a sandwich with an odd mixture of fillings, e.g. mayonnaise and jam, mustard and banana, chutney and marmalade.

93 MAKE A COLLAGE

* **NUMBER OF PLAYERS:** Minimum: Eight
  Maximum: As many as can be fitted into the room available

* **PLAYED BY SMALL GROUPS OF BETWEEN FOUR AND EIGHT PEOPLE**

* **ACCOMMODATION:** Enough space to accommodate the number of groups. If necessary, this can be in more than one room

* **PREPARATION AND EQUIPMENT:** A large sheet of paper (at least A3, but preferably larger) and a bag for each group containing (each bag containing the same):
  * Pair of scissors
  * Glue and/or Blu-Tack™
  * One or more felt-tipped pens
  * A selection of any or all of the following:
    ○ Crêpe paper
    ○ Brown wrapping paper
    ○ Pictorial gift-wrapping paper
    ○ Birthday cards
    ○ Pieces of material
    ○ Cotton wool
    ○ Balls or strands of wool
    ○ Glitter
    ○ Sandpaper
    ○ Drinking straws

* **PLAYERS TO KNOW EACH OTHER WELL:** Not necessary, but it can add to the fun if they do

EACH TEAM IS GIVEN A BAG AND ASKED TO PRODUCE A COLLAGE DEPICTING THE ACTIVITIES OF THEIR GROUP. TYPICAL GROUPS THAT MIGHT BE REPRESENTED: CHURCH, HOUSE GROUP, GOLF CLUB, WOMEN'S INSTITUTE, WALKING GROUP – OR EVEN THEIR FAMILY.

They are given about 20 minutes to complete the task, though if longer is requested by all or a majority of the team members, then allow it.

When completed the collages are displayed and all players vote on the best by marking it with a tick. They cannot, of course, tick their own collage!!

94 WHEN THE REVOLUTION COMES (OR IF I RULED THE WORLD)

* *NUMBER OF PLAYERS:* Minimum: 12
  Maximum: 25

* *PLAYED BY INDIVIDUALS (BUT NON-COMPETITIVE)*

* *PREPARATION AND EQUIPMENT:* None

* *ACCOMMODATION:* Enough room for all present to sit in an approximate circle

* *PLAYERS TO KNOW EACH OTHER WELL:* Not necessary

This is a non-competitive game in which each person in turn states one law they would pass or one thing they would ban or one thing they would introduce if, 'when the revolution comes', they ruled the world. It is not meant to be an occasion for mentioning the major things we would all like to see happen, such as hunger eliminated, cancer conquered or everyone becoming Christians, but more to tackle lesser annoyances or nuisances.

Examples of things said when this game has been played are:

• Ban making long calls on mobile phones on a train
• Make property developers move in opposite their own developments
• Bar background music in shops
• Don't allow travel companies to raise their prices during school holidays

95 CREATE A GRAFFITI WALL

* *NUMBER OF PLAYERS:* Minimum: Ten
Maximum: No limit

* *PLAYED BY INDIVIDUALS*

* *ACCOMMODATION:* Large room or hall with a blank wall on which it is acceptable to stick a large length of paper

* *PREPARATION AND EQUIPMENT:* Length of kitchen paper or smooth wallpaper, at least six feet long; selection of thick felt-tip pens or magic markers

* *PLAYERS TO KNOW EACH OTHER WELL:* Not necessary

....

THIS IS NOT A COMPETITIVE GAME, BUT AN OPPORTUNITY FOR PEOPLE TO DO A BIT OF GRAFFITI QUITE LEGALLY!

The paper should be left on the wall throughout the party and people encouraged from time to time to go and do their bit. Their contributions can be written or drawn, copied or original.

At the end of the party, take a few moments for everyone to come up to it and admire all the work.

96 READING NO. 1 – ARE YOU GETTING OLD?

How do you know when you are getting old?

- Everything hurts – and what doesn't hurt doesn't work.
- The gleam in your eye is the sun glinting on your bifocals.
- You feel like the morning after, but haven't been anywhere.
- You get winded playing cards.
- Your children begin to look middle-aged.
- You join a health club but don't go.
- A dripping tap causes an uncontrollable urge.
- You know all the answers but nobody asks you the questions.
- You look forward to a dull evening.
- You need glasses to find your glasses.
- You turn out the light for economy, instead of romance.
- You sit in a rocking chair, but can't make it go.
- Your knees buckle but your belt won't.
- Your back goes out more than you do.
- You put your bra on back to front and it fits better.
- Your house is too big and your medicine chest not big enough.
- You sink your teeth into a steak and they stay there.
- Your birthday cake collapses under the weight of the candles.
- You have to find a child to open your childproof pill containers for you.

… And, inevitably, the two most certain signs are:

- You lose your short-term memory…
- And I can't remember what the second one is.

97 READING NO. 2 – WHY DID THE CHICKEN CROSS THE ROAD?

L.A. Police Department:
Give us five minutes with the chicken and we'll find out.

———————

Richard M. Nixon:
The chicken did not cross the road. I repeat, the chicken did *not* cross the road. I don't know any chickens. I have never known any chickens.

———————

Dr Seuss:
Did the chicken cross the road?
Did he cross it with a toad?
Yes! The chicken crossed the road, but why it crossed, I've not been told!

———————

Colonel Sanders:
I missed one?

———————

Martin Luther King, Jr:
I envision a world where all chickens will be free to cross roads without having their motives called into question.

———————

Grandpa:
In my day, we didn't ask why the chicken crossed the road. Someone told us that the chicken crossed the road, and that was good enough for us.

———————

Aristotle:
It is the nature of chickens to cross the road.

Saddam Hussein:
This was an unprovoked act of rebellion and we were quite justified in dropping 50 tons of nerve gas on it.

———————

Captain James T. Kirk:
To boldly go where no chicken has gone before.

———————

Freud:
The fact that you are at all concerned that the chicken crossed the road reveals your underlying sexual insecurity.

———————

Bill Gates:
I have just released Chicken Coop 2008, which will not only cross roads, but will lay eggs, file your important documents and balance your cheque book, and it can be installed on both Windows XP and Vista.

———————

Einstein:
Did the chicken really cross the road or did the road move beneath the chicken?

———————

Bill Clinton:
I did not cross the road with THAT chicken. However, I did ask Vernon Jordan to find the chicken a job in New York.

———————

The Bible:
And God looked down from the heavens, and He said unto the chicken, 'Thou shalt cross the road.' And the chicken crossed the road, and there was much rejoicing.

READING NO. 3 – CHURCH NOTICES

HERE IS A SELECTION OF CHURCH NOTICES THAT HAVE NOT BEEN WORDED IN THE BEST WAY!

The preacher for next Sunday will be found hanging in the porch.

As it is Easter Sunday, we will ask Mrs Smith to come and lay an egg on the altar.

The topic for next Sunday evening will be 'What is hell?' Come early and hear our choir practise.

This is the vicar's last Sunday with us. The choir will sing a special anthem, 'Break forth with joy'.

Will those attending the Weight Watchers group please use the large double doors at the side of the hall.

Don't let worry kill you. Let the church help.

If you don't know what sin is, come to one of our services.

On Tuesday evening there will be an ice-cream social. All ladies giving milk, please come early.

The ladies of the church have cast off clothing of every kind. They may be seen in the church basement every Friday.

The pastor is on vacation. Massages can be given to the church secretary.

Could all missionary collecting boxes be returned by Friday as the vicar is going on holiday on Saturday?

The choir invites any member of the congregation who enjoys sinning to join the choir.

_____

For those of you who have children and don't know it, we have a crèche downstairs.

_____

Ladies, don't forget the rummage sale. It's a chance to get rid of those things not worth keeping around the house. Bring your husbands.

_____

We will be meeting in the town square on Friday to pray for rain. If wet, in the church hall.

_____

Remember in prayer the many who are sick of our church and community.

_____

During the absence of our pastor, we enjoyed the rare privilege of hearing a good sermon when A. B. Doe supplied our pulpit.

_____

The Rev. Adams spoke briefly, much to the delight of his audience.

_____

Irving Benson and Jessie Carter were married on 24 October in the church. So ends a friendship that began in their school days.

_____

Miss Charlene Mason sang 'I will not pass this way again', giving obvious pleasure to the congregation.

_____

The healing service due to be held tomorrow has been cancelled owing to the illness of the vicar.

_____

The group for those suffering from low self-esteem will meet in the church room tomorrow. Please use the rear side entrance.

_____

The installation of a new font at the front of the church means babies can now be baptized at both ends.

_____

The sermon this morning will be 'Jesus walks on water'.
The sermon tonight will be 'Searching for Jesus'.

Please place your donation in the envelope along with the deceased person you want remembered.

———————

Next Thursday there will be tryouts for the choir. They need all the help they can get.

———————

The cost for this week's 'Fasting and Prayer' conference includes meals.

———————

The third verse of the hymn will be sung without musical accomplishment.

———————

The concert held in the church hall was a great success. Special thanks are due to Mrs Rice, who laboured all evening at the piano, which, as usual, fell on her.

———————

If you want to know more about sin, come to our church.

99 *YOUR OWN PANTO*

This is a spoof on *Cinderella*. The idea is that it should be played absolutely deadpan and all the parts, with the possible exception of the narrator, taken by men. Although all the players should be able to look through their scripts in advance, there is no need to rehearse or learn lines as they will be reading from their scripts.

Players: Narrator
           Cinderella
           Two ugly sisters
           Prince Charming
           The fairy godmother

It adds to the fun if the players can find some appropriate items of costume or props, though these are not strictly necessary.

For example, when a walking group did this, they used a walking pole for the fairy godmother's magic wand and a walking boot for the glass slipper.

....

NARRATOR: I recently came across an old manuscript of the pantomime *Cinderella*. In complete contrast to many modern productions, this version is unashamedly touching and romantic. I think we may allow ourselves to revel in its old-fashioned values, and let us not be embarrassed if it moves us to tears.

INTRODUCTION

CINDERELLA: I am Cinderella. I am beautiful.
PRINCE: I am Prince Charming. I am handsome.
UGLY SISTERS: We are the ugly sisters. We are ugly.
FAIRY GODMOTHER: I am the fairy godmother. I am good.

SCENE 1 – THE KITCHEN OF A GRAND HOUSE

SISTERS: We are going to the ball. We are happy.
CINDERELLA: I am not going to the ball. I am sad.
SISTERS: Help us get ready for the ball.
CINDERELLA: All right.
SISTER 1:   Fetch my gown.
CINDERELLA: All right.
SISTER 2:   Clean my shoes.
CINDERELLA: All right.
SISTER 1:   Brush my hair.
CINDERELLA: All right.
SISTER 2:   Wipe my nose.
CINDERELLA: All right.
SISTER 1:   Have my cocoa ready when I get back.
CINDERELLA: All right.
SISTER 2:   And put a hot water bottle in my bed.
CINDERELLA: All right.
CINDERELLA: They have gone. I am sad.

SCENE 2 – THE SAME PLACE ONE HOUR LATER

CINDERELLA: I am still sad because I am not going to the ball.
FAIRY GODMOTHER: Hello. I am your fairy godmother. Would you like to go to the ball?
CINDERELLA: All right.
GODMOTHER: Fetch me a pumpkin…
CINDERELLA: All right.
GODMOTHER: …and six mice.

CINDERELLA:	All right.
GODMOTHER:	Here is your coach and now I will give you a beautiful ball gown. Do you like it?
CINDERELLA:	All right.
GODMOTHER:	You must be home before midnight.
CINDERELLA:	All right.

SCENE 3 – THE ROYAL PALACE

UGLY SISTERS:	The prince hasn't danced with us. We are sad.
PRINCE:	There are no pretty girls here. I am sad. Oh, a pretty one has just arrived.
PRINCE:	[addressing Cinderella] Dance?
CINDERELLA:	All right.
PRINCE:	I love her. I am happy.
CINDERELLA:	I love him. I am happy.
SISTERS:	He still hasn't danced with us. We are sad.
NARRATOR:	Chime, chime, chime, chime…
CINDERELLA:	Oh dear, it is midnight. I must go.
PRINCE:	May I see you again?
CINDERELLA:	All right.
PRINCE:	She has dropped her slipper.

SCENE 4 – THE KITCHEN THE FOLLOWING DAY

NARRATOR:	Ring, ring…
SISTERS:	Cinderella, answer the door.
CINDERELLA:	All right.
PRINCE:	I will marry the girl this slipper fits. [Sister 1 tries it on]
SISTER 1:	It fits.
PRINCE:	No, it doesn't. [Sister 2 struggles to get it on]
SISTER 2:	It fits.
PRINCE:	No, it doesn't. [Cinderella tries it on]

CINDERELLA:	It fits.
PRINCE:	Marry me?
CINDERELLA:	All right.

EPILOGUE

CINDERELLA:	I am happy.
PRINCE:	I am married.
SISTERS:	We are still ugly and still sad.
GODMOTHER:	I am still good.
NARRATOR:	So everything ended up 'all right'!

100 ALL MEMBERS OF ONE BODY

Finally, a sketch describing different ministries in the church, in which the players break in on each other's words and it ends up as hilarious nonsense.

A sample sketch is given below, but it would need to be adapted to suit your own group.

....

Organizer announces:

'We thought it would be a good thing to take the opportunity to share with you all a little background to the ministries we are involved in at St John's/Bethel/Bridge Street. We have Brian representing the Maintenance Team and Jean the Seniors' Day Centre, Vicki reporting on our rambling and travel group, Shirley on working in the Parish Office and Hilary explaining about the Prayer Ministry Team.'

SHIRLEY: As the workload in the office has increased, we decided to recruit a new member of staff. The sort of person we needed would be...

JEAN: ...over 70 and able to eat her meals without them being mashed or liquidized. We have been pleased to welcome two new helpers, one of whom was…

BRIAN: ...covered in rust and needed rubbing down and rust-proofing. We have had some concern about the plumbing at the vicarage and felt that what was needed was…

HILARY: ...laying-on of hands and deep ministry. Members of the Ministry Team are asked to always come...

VICKI: ...equipped with walking boots and wet-weather wear. We have been pleased to welcome several new members recently, who...

SHIRLEY: ...were photocopied, stapled together and circulated to the Standing Committee.

JEAN: In the Day Centre we always try to provide a good nutritious meal. A great favourite is treacle pudding served with...

BRIAN: ...magnolia paint. Some members of the Maintenance Team have been involved in the construction of the new baptismal pool. This will soon be ready for use and filled with...

JEAN: ...tomato soup. We run lots of activities for our members and during the past year the old people have enjoyed...

VICKI: ...river rafting, paragliding and mountain biking. We also went on a cycle ride to a delightful old village, where the houses were all...

JEAN: ...covered in cheese sauce, which we always find...

SHIRLEY: ...very useful to keep the photocopier running smoothly. We get lots of telephone enquiries in the office. The other day someone asked if we could tell her where she could find...

HILARY: ...healing for the memory of...

BRIAN: ...being suspended upside down in the belfry...

HILARY: Another woman felt she needed inner healing after being…

SHIRLEY: …packaged up and posted to the Bishop of the Diocese, who…

VICKI: …joined the rest of us for a sandwich lunch. If anyone can't manage the whole walk, we arrange for them to be…

BRIAN: …stripped down, sandpapered all over and sprayed with bright green paint.

HILARY: Sometimes it seems right to anoint people with…

SHIRLEY: …Tippex™. It can get very noisy in the office, especially when they are experimenting with the sound system in the church, but we don't let this worry us. We simply plug up our ears with…

JEAN: …baked beans.

VICKI: On our walks we often stop at a café and indulge ourselves with tea and cakes. Recently we enjoyed some particularly interesting confections, which were rather like…

BRIAN: …set concrete. The Maintenance Team keeps very busy and every Wednesday morning you will see us all busily…

JEAN: …knitting blanket squares…

HILARY: …for those suffering from…

BRIAN: …blocked pipes.

HILARY: When there is a large number of people wanting ministry, we find the best thing is to…

SHIRLEY: …fix them to the wall with Blu-Tack™.

VICKI: The next walk will be on 12 July, when you are invited to join us with…

JEAN: …a Zimmer frame…

BRIAN: …a bucket of compost…

HILARY: …a large box of tissues…

SHIRLEY: …and a copy of the Stewards' Rota.

An alternative is to take people's everyday occupations and write a script along similar lines. This has been done with the following: a doctor, a builder, a nursery school teacher, a vicar and a dental technician.

ADDITIONAL GAMES

101 VALENTINE'S DAY (A QUIZ ABOUT LOVE AND LOVERS)

* **NUMBER OF PLAYERS:** Any number

* **PLAYED BY INDIVIDUALS, PAIRS OR SMALL GROUPS**

* **ACCOMMODATION:** Enough room for all present

* **PREPARATION AND EQUIPMENT:** Photocopied list and pen or pencil for each group, pair or individual player

* **PLAYERS TO KNOW EACH OTHER WELL:** Not necessary

....

1. 25 and 50 years are the silver and golden wedding anniversaries, but what is the one-year anniversary?
2. In which play do the lines 'If music be the food of love, play on' appear?
3. In which musical show does the following song occur : 'I'm in love with a wonderful guy'?
4. …and which character sang that song?
5. And in which musical was the song 'Hello, young lovers'?
6. In which chapter of the Bible is the well-known passage on love ('Though I speak with the tongues of men and of angels…')?
7. How many times was Elizabeth Taylor married?
8. Who was the first husband of Marilyn Monroe?
9. Whom did C. S. Lewis marry?
10. 'Love and marriage, love and marriage, go together like …' complete the line of this song.
11. Who was Jacob's favourite wife?
12. How many wives is a Muslim man permitted?

13. What is the term for a wife who has several husbands: 'poly...'?
14. Who built the Taj Mahal in memory of his much-loved wife?
15. Lovers sometimes put the letters 'S W A L K' on the back of an envelope. What do they mean?
16. Fill in the missing word in the song: 'Love is a many- .... thing'.
17. Who was King David's first wife?
18. Which modern-day musical is based on the Shakespeare play *Romeo and Juliet*?
19. Who sang the song 'April Love'?
20. To whom was Aquila married?

ANSWERS TO 'VALENTINE'S DAY (A QUIZ ABOUT LOVE AND LOVERS)'

1. Cotton or paper
2. Twelfth Night
3. South Pacific
4. Nellie Forbush
5. The King and I
6. 1 Corinthians 13
7. Eight
8. Joe di Maggio
9. Joy Gresham
10. A horse and carriage
11. Rachel
12. Four
13. Polyandry
14. Emperor Shah Jahan
15. Sealed with a loving kiss
16. splendored
17. Michal
18. West Side Story
19. Pat Boone
20. Priscilla

102 *RUN WHEN YOU HEAR IT*

* **NUMBER OF PLAYERS:** Minimum: 20 (two teams of ten+)
  Maximum: No limit

* **PLAYED IN TEAMS**

* **ACCOMMODATION:** Large room

* **PREPARATION AND EQUIPMENT:** Sufficient chairs for each team to be
   seated, plus one more chair; a story for the organizer to read
   out

* **PLAYERS TO KNOW EACH OTHER WELL:** Not necessary

....

THIS IS A GAME FOR ANY GROUP OF PEOPLE WHO BELONG TO SOMETHING – A SOCIAL CLUB, A SPORTS TEAM, A CHURCH, ETC. EACH MEMBER OF EACH TEAM IS GIVEN A NAME, PLACE OR ACTIVITY CONNECTED WITH THAT GROUP.

e.g. for a church: Sunday, service, the minister's name, the sermon, the choir, music group, kids' club, youth group, Mothers' union, coffee bar, Sunday services, bookstall, stewards, deacons, church council, homegroups.

For a golf club: the course, the clubhouse, tournaments, the greenkeeper, the team captain, the flag, the rough, caddies, winner, birdie, eagle.

Tennis club: the courts, sets, racquets, singles, doubles, balls, match, net, umpire, tournaments, winner, rained off.

Art group: paint, draw, exhibition, brushes, models, picture frames, sales, beginners, sketching.

_____

The teams sit on chairs with the first person in the team about ten feet away from another chair.

The organizer starts to tell a story. When he/she mentions the name of the whole group, e.g. St John's Church, Newtown Golf Club, etc., all the members in each team get up, run round the chair in front and back to their own place. The first team to have all members seated back on their chairs gets a point.

When he/she mentions a particular item (i.e. the choir or the clubhouse), the team members given that word get up, run round the chair in front and go back to their places. Again, the first member back gets a point for his/her team.

_____

Typical story:
St John's church is on the outskirts of the town and its minister is Rev. Peter Walker. Their morning service is at 10.30 on Sunday morning, and at the same time as the main service a kids' club is run for the younger members of St John's. There are many other activities during the week, including homegroups, the Mothers' Union and a youth group. The minister is particularly involved with the youth group, encouraging them to start their own music group, for which the church council put up a sum of money for instruments. Now the St John's music group is in demand from other churches in the town, to the great delight of the minister, the church council and the members of St John's. They also have a very good choir, which draws its members from all ages of the congregation of St John's, especially the Mothers' Union and the many homegroups. Both the choir and the music group take part in the Sunday services at St John's. After the service the members usually stay on to enjoy a cup of coffee at the coffee bar, and parents are reunited there with their children, who are eager to report on what they have been doing at kids' club, and the choir members, who have got a bit dry with their singing efforts, particularly appreciate the service provided by the coffee

bar. Meeting at the <u>coffee bar</u> is a good occasion for <u>homegroup</u> members to get to know people from other <u>homegroups</u> and indeed for all the members of <u>St John's</u> to enjoy fellowship and perhaps have a chat with the <u>minister</u>.

103 WHAT DOES IT STAND FOR?

✳ *NUMBER OF PLAYERS:* Minimum: Six
Maximum: 15

✳ *PLAYED BY INDIVIDUALS*

✳ *ACCOMMODATION:* Room to accommodate the number of players

✳ *PREPARATION AND EQUIPMENT:* For each player, a pen or pencil and a sheet of paper

✳ *PLAYERS TO KNOW EACH OTHER WELL:* Not necessary, but it is more fun if they do

The organizer calls out a word – a place or name or other word, preferably one appropriate to those present, e.g.:

- London
- Baseball
- St Paul's
- John Ball

Players are then asked to write this word down the left-hand side of their paper, one letter on each line, and are then asked to make a suitable sentence or acronym out of all the letters.

E.g.:

- **L**ook
- **O**ver
- **N**ew

- **Designs**
- **Of**
- **Nightdresses**

- **John**
- **Only**
- **Happy**
- **Nibbling**

- **Buns**
- **At**
- **Local**
- **Launderette**

After 15 minutes, the papers are laid out and the players reward the one they think is best with a star – not their own, of course!

104 CHURCH JOKES

A minister asked his congregation to read a Bible passage in preparation for his sermon the following week and gave them the reference: Mark 21.

When the next Sunday came, he asked all those who had read the passage to raise their hands. Nearly the entire congregation did so.

'Right,' he said, 'as there *is* no chapter 21 in Mark's Gospel, my sermon will be on the subject of lying.'

It was the day after the wedding at Cana and Simon Peter was in bed with a terrible hangover. 'Is there anything I can get you?' asked his wife. 'Yes,' he replied. 'A glass of water, but, whatever you do, don't let HIM get his hands on it.'

A very devout Catholic lady had been praying about something for some time without apparently getting any answer. Finally, in exasperation she said, 'Lord, if you don't give me an answer, I shall go and tell your mother.'

Four ministers met regularly for a time of prayer and sharing.

One week one of them said, 'I have something I want to confess to you all, which is really weighing me down. I am a secret drinker and have a real problem with alcohol.'

The second one then said, 'Well, as our brother has confessed his great weakness, I think I should let you all know that I have a great problem with gambling. No one in my church knows, but I'm really addicted.'

The third one said, 'Well, as it seems to be the time for confession, I must tell you all that I have a problem with women. I just can't resist a pretty girl.'

They all turned to the fourth minister. 'And do you have a secret sin, brother?'

'Oh yes,' he replied. 'I'm a compulsive gossip.'

When old Bridie came into the church to pray, a couple of workmen on the roof thought they'd have a bit of fun with her.

'Hello,' one of them called down. 'This is God.'

Bridie took no notice, but went on praying 'Hail Mary...'

Again one of them called, 'Hello, this is God speaking.'

Once more Bridie took no notice and continued 'Hail Mary...'

However, when one of the men called out for the third time, 'This is God', she looked up and said reprovingly, 'Will you please not interrupt when I'm speaking to your mother!'

A visiting preacher came to a church and, as the people filed out at the end of the service, a number of them thanked him and told him what a wonderful sermon he had preached. He felt very gratified, until a man came up and said, 'That was the worst sermon I've heard in years.'

'Don't worry about him,' said the churchwarden standing nearby. 'He's a bit simple and doesn't know what he's talking about. He just repeats what he's heard other people say.'

The vicar was taking the funeral of an elderly lady, whose relatives had asked that at the end of the service he would play a song from *The Wizard of Oz*. They gave the vicar a CD, which he passed on to the verger, who set it at the right place to play. However, when the vicar pressed the button, instead of 'Somewhere over the Rainbow' it started to play the song 'Ding, dong, the wicked witch is dead'. (Reputedly true!)

Fed up with mopping up the result of leaks that had appeared in the ark, Noah's wife complained to him, 'If only you hadn't insisted on bringing those two woodworms!'